I'm Listening, Lord

To Diana,
Keep Listening!

Marilyn Heavilin
Ps 46:10

I'm Listening, Lord

Marilyn Willett Heavilin

THOMAS NELSON PUBLISHERS
Nashville

Published in Nashville, Tennessee, by Thomas Nelson, Inc., Publishers, and distributed in Canada by Word Communications, Ltd., Richmond, British Columbia, and in the United Kingdom by Word (UK), Ltd., Milton Keynes, England.

Unless otherwise noted, Scripture quotations are from THE NEW KING JAMES VERSION. Copyright © 1979, 1980, 1982, Thomas Nelson, Inc., Publishers.

Scripture quotations noted TLB are from *The Living Bible* (Wheaton, Illinois: Tyndale House Publishers, 1971) and are used by permission.

Scripture quotations noted NIV are taken from the HOLY BIBLE, NEW INTERNATIONAL VERSION®. Copyright © 1973, 1978, 1984 by International Bible Society. Used by permission of Zondervan Bible Publishing House. All rights reserved.

The "NIV" and "New International Version" trademarks are registered in the United States Patent and Trademark Office by International Bible Society. Use of either trademark requires the permission of International Bible Society.

Scripture quotations noted KJV are from The Holy Bible, KING JAMES VERSION.

Scripture quotations noted NASB are from THE NEW AMERICAN STANDARD BIBLE, Copyright © 1960, 1962, 1963, 1968, 1971, 1972, 1973, 1975, 1977 by The Lockman Foundation and are used by permission.

Library of Congress Cataloging-in-Publication Data

Heavilin, Marilyn Willett.
  I'm listening, Lord / Marilyn Willett Heavilin.
    p. cm.
  Includes biographical references.
  ISBN 0-8407-3497-2 (pbk.)
  1. Prayer—Christianity. I. Title
  BV215.H47 1993   93-24103
  248.3′2—dc20   CIP

Printed in the United States of America
1 2 3 4 5 6 7 - 98 97 96 95 94 93

To

Katie Spencer

who encouraged me to stretch

just a little bit more

Contents

Part 4: The Purpose of Prayer

Part 5: The Process of Prayer

Part 6: The Product of Prayer

Foreword

I suppose that most forewords are written *after* the fact. The author presents a finished manuscript for one to read, to become acquainted with, and finally to introduce to you the reader.

This foreword is different, for I have been privileged to see its message unfold and fully "fleshed out" in Marilyn Heavilin's life years before any of us thought it would take the form of a book. After all—because the Word became flesh, and because Jesus lives in His people—the fullest and most rounded knowledge is now always "incarnational," and never again to be relegated to the merely abstract or theoretical.

I met Marilyn and her husband, Glen, some five years ago at our church, soon deepening our fellowship in a couples small group Bible study. I was immediately aware of Marilyn's big heart for the living God, and for people, especially troubled people.

As a practicing psychiatrist, I was intrigued by Marilyn's keen discernment and insight into people, and came to know her life story of growth and victory through grief and loss. She was already speaking to thousands across the country, and "naturally" (by divine appointment) came into contact with hundreds of inquiring and troubled people. It seemed that the Lord was teaching a number of us more about prayer, especially about what Marilyn, in this book, calls "two-way prayer," speaking *and* listening to Him. We fell in step as the Lord taught us, and I have been deeply influenced by the author as a model for availability to God and His people for prayer. For several years now, we have often worked together as a team to pray with people, to walk with them into His presence, there to express the deepest things of their lives and to hear and deeply receive His healing and encouraging words.

Even as I read the manuscript, I knew immediately that I wanted to give this book to a growing number of specific people: a young man recently graduated from college and struggling with identity and longing to know the Lord better. A Hispanic woman who comes to group therapy in my clinic and who is learning to open up to trusted people and to God the deepest things of her heart. A number of couples who are essentially emerging from various forms of "toxic religion" and who need sound, clear, scriptural wisdom as they restore the loving dialogue with the Father which is the birthright and destiny of every son and daughter of the King. A Vietnam vet who seems to be losing his wife and family just as he emerges from several years of the deepest depression, discouragement, and anxiety. A number of women who are working through the pain, shame, fear, and isolation of early life abuse, but who need to keep doing so in a grounded theocentric, Christocentric way, so that their recovery is anchored in the living and written Word of God.

But this book is not just for the most troubled, but equally for those who "merely" need to grow in prayer, who need to be refocused and reinvigorated to pray without ceasing during these incredible 1990s and beyond.

I believe this book fits into a widening and deepening stream of truth which the Lord is actively restoring to His people as He renews and cleanses us. We who know Him are called to fellowship with Him, to worship, *listen*, and obey. We have known these things, of course, and in a sense this book will remind us of things we've known. But like the disciples at Gethsemane, we have grown weary or fallen asleep in the doing.

Like most really good communication, this book is deceptively simple. It artfully and modestly conceals the hard work, carefully crafted outline and infrastructure study, prayer, sweat, and labor of love the author put into it. It lucidly calls us back to simple, practical truth: to a naturally supernatural, disciplined, spontaneous, rational, wholehearted walking, talking, listening, and obeying the Savior. If anything, it runs the risk of having its very simplicity mislead the superficial reader about its depth.

This book arrives after being prayed out, cried out, studied out, walked out, praised out, and lived out for much more than a decade of its author's life. It arrives, I believe, at a strategic, epochal time, to recall the Wuest translation's rendering of the Greek word for "time," *kairos,* for which we have no exact word in English.

For, you see, this book is also a timely translation of truths from the heart of God, through the author's patient, obedient life-grasp of Scripture, learned in His presence, which will be refreshing and encouraging for a great variety of readers. I believe God is preparing His people for renewal. He is readying us to be the people of His presence in and for our times. As we love and know Jesus, may He love His world through us. May God use this book, and you, and all of its readers beyond all that we ask or think, for His purposes, joy, and glory!

John I. Benson, M.D.
Redlands, California

To the Reader

Several years ago a friend approached me to ask if I would present a weekend seminar on prayer. The request seemed overwhelming to me since I had never presented even a single message on the topic, and yet I admitted I was intrigued with the idea.

Over the previous few years prayer had become increasingly important in my own life. After the death of my seventeen-year-old son, Nathan, I spent an increased amount of time talking to God. Notice I said talking "to," not necessarily talking "with," God. Much of the time I felt my prayers went no further than the ceiling and then came bouncing back—pieces of my own questions and requests falling unanswered all around me.

After a long period of grieving, I had the opportunity to spend an entire day in prayer for emotional healing. During that day I began to get in touch with God again. My dry spell of ineffective prayer was ended—at least for a while. For the next few years I had long periods where I felt God really heard me, and then interludes when I felt my prayer life was shallow and meaningless.

During one of those periods a friend suggested I try writing my prayers. What a wise suggestion. With my head, heart, and hand all working in unison, I seldom have to struggle with lack of concentration or problems of other interruptions. I keep a small notebook near me to jot down the intrusive but important thoughts that always pop into my mind when I'm trying to focus on God: *Remember to pick up the cleaning; you have to make plane reservations today; it's Mary's birthday;* etc., etc. I allow my answering machine to collect my phone calls, and if by chance I do need to take a call, since the prayer is written, I know right where I left off.

As I shared my prayer progress with my friend, she encouraged me even more to do a workshop on prayer for her church, and I agreed. At that seminar I presented four messages on the power, purpose, process, and product of prayer. Nearly a hundred people attended the two-day seminar, and many of them told me that they developed a new appreciation for and an understanding of prayer at that seminar. The old adage is true that the teacher often learns more than the students, and I suspect it was true in my case, also. As I studied deeply what God's Word says about prayer, my desire to develop a deeper prayer life myself increased. I continued to read and study on my own and since then I have also attended several prayer seminars conducted by noted Christian leaders.

As I have continued to write in my prayer journal, God has added a new dimension to the writing of my prayers. As I have trained my ear to hear and know His voice, I have begun writing down what God says to me in my personal prayer time. Now I am not just talking "to" God; I am conversing "with" Him. After all of these years I have discovered God meant prayer to be a two-way interaction. Now I can hardly wait for that special time when I can record what my Father is saying to me.

The verse, "Be still, and know that I am God" (Ps. 46:10) has taken on a fuller meaning for me. I now realize God has often attempted to speak to me, but I was too busy talking and was never quiet enough to hear His voice. Jeremiah quotes God, "I spoke to you, . . . but you did not hear, and I called you, but you did not answer" (Jer. 7:13). The sovereign Lord is waiting to speak with each of His children if we are willing to listen.

After speaking at a weekend retreat in Southern California, I received this note from Irma:

In my journal my prayers come alive. Like the epistles, they tell a story; a history of my walk with Him; of my victories and struggles.

While I have been journaling my prayers for a long time, it wasn't until I heard you speak at my church retreat that I started recording His answers to me. My prayer journal and life will never be the same.

The impact has come along three lines:

1. Consistency—His voice has given me a hunger to pray and seek Him daily.

2. Intercessory prayer—"It is not that we bring God into touch with our minds, but that we rouse ourselves until God is able to convey His mind to us about the one for whom we intercede" (Oswald Chambers, *My Utmost for His Highest*, March 31).

3. Psychological health—His name is Counselor. In my journal, I have found, as I pour out my hurt and confusion, He is there with direction, focus, and comfort in a concrete way. It is a gift which He gives abundantly.

IT WORKS!!

Most of us are very comfortable letting God speak to us through His Word, through circumstances, and through other Christians. However, we're not as comfortable with God speaking to us directly. Oswald Chambers states:

We show how little we love God by preferring to listen to His servants only. We like to listen to personal testimonies, but we do not desire that God Himself should speak to us. Why are we so terrified lest God should speak to us? Because we know that if God does speak, either the thing must be done or we must tell God we will not obey Him.[1]

I agree with Chambers that when others give us advice, we feel we can choose whether to take the advice or not. However, when God speaks, we know our options are limited. Recently I did a workshop on listening prayer at the Southern California Women's Retreat in La

Jolla, California. Afterward, a young woman asked for my advice to resolve a problem between her and her husband. Our time was limited, and there was no absolute answer to her question, so I suggested she spend time writing in her journal, asking God what to do, and listening for His direction. A few weeks later I received a card from her.

> I just wanted to let you know that you helped me learn how to hear from God. I began to realize that I was not putting my husband or marriage in God's divine order of things. Well, I am now, and I decided to attend my husband's church with him on Sundays. I feel a great peace with my decision and my marriage is wonderful! I even got flowers! The card read "From the two guys who will love you forever" (my husband and God!). Thank you for helping me learn to hear from God! My marriage thanks you, too!—Julie

I have been encouraged to see the recent increased interest in prayer in our society. The cover of *Newsweek* magazine, January 6, 1992, read: "Talking to God, An Intimate Look at the Way We Pray." The National and International Religion Report, 1992, presented a special report by David Bryant entitled "The Most Hopeful Sign of Our Times: A Growing Prayer Movement Points America Toward Spiritual Revival." In a recent readers' poll conducted by *Christianity Today*, a book on prayer was chosen to receive the top award as the book of the year for 1993.

Although a new interest in prayer definitely seems to be moving across this country, I believe there is still a general lack of understanding concerning prayer. In preparation for writing this book, this year I conducted a survey on prayer among my audiences. When I started to compose the survey, I wrote the question: "How often do you spend more than fifteen minutes at one time in prayer? Several times a day _____, Daily _____, Every other day _____, Weekly _____, Monthly _____, Other _____." As I wrote it, I felt the Lord saying, "Change that to five minutes."

I thought, *People will be offended if I suggest they might be spending only five minutes a day in prayer.* However, I followed the Lord's prompting and changed fifteen to five.

You can imagine my surprise as I started to tabulate the surveys. Only a handful marked that they pray more than five minutes at a time several times a day. Fewer than half said that they pray more than five minutes at a time at least once a day.

A small portion of those surveyed said they felt they have heard God's voice, but even fewer felt they knew how to tell if what they heard was genuine. After seeing the results of this survey, I am more convinced than ever that the laity, and perhaps even the clergy, need some motivation to develop a satisfying prayer life—which I hope to provide—but I also realize we need to talk about the barriers to an effective prayer life and how we can know when we truly hear God's voice. All of these topics will be discussed in this book.

However, I believe one area must come even before we discuss the barriers to prayer and how we can learn to recognize God's voice. Those of you who have read my other books will recall that as I walked through the deaths of three of my sons, I heard many views on God. I have discovered that most Christians have created God in their own image. We have decided what attributes we want our God to have, and then we serve the God we have created. Therefore, our image of God often does not line up with the God described in Scripture, our one authorized link to a valid presentation of God. A wrong concept of God causes us to develop a lopsided concept of prayer—one where all of our requests are granted our way, and we talk and God listens.

Most Christians today know God only as Savior, and their relationship with Him stops there. Those who have dared to try to know God as more than Savior often still limit themselves to the attributes of God that are comfortable and easy to integrate into their preconceived image of God. We will always have wrong expectations of prayer if we do not know the God of Scripture, the true Principal of prayer. Therefore, in the following chapters we will discuss how we can get to know God on an intimate and authentic basis, and then I will share with you what I believe are some very exciting concepts on prayer.

This book is designed to be a one-step-at-a-time handbook that will help you develop your own individual, satisfying dialogue with God.

May God richly bless you as you not only learn to talk with Him more effectively, but also as you learn to listen while God speaks to you.

For Reflection

1. Take some time right now to list at least ten adjectives you would use to describe God.

   Omnipotent, Omnipresent,
   (all powerful) (Everywhere at once)
   Loving, Caring, Wise,
   Patient, Forgiving

2. Now list your own personal reasons for praying.

   To connect with my creator.
   To express thanks for blessings.
   To share my hopes, fears, needs.
   To ask for help.

Part

1

GOD,
THE PRINCIPAL OF
PRAYER

1

Know the Principal of Prayer

Before we can develop an effective prayer life, we must learn to really know God, the Principal of prayer. When I speak of knowing God, I'm not referring just to receiving Jesus Christ as our personal Savior. I am also speaking of knowing His personality and His perspective. The only way we can know Him in this way is to study Scripture and find out what it says about God—our Savior, our Provider, and the One to whom we pray.

In southern California I often see a bumper sticker which says, "God is a Good God." As I read it, my reaction is always the same, "Yes, but. . . ." I sense the writer of that statement is critiquing God by his own understanding of the word *good*, which most likely means "everything that will make me happy."

Many years ago, my husband and I listened to a well-known pastor explain his position on marriage after a divorce. He explained that he felt it must be all right for people to marry again after they had been divorced because he was certain God wouldn't want them to be unhappy for the rest of their lives. Please note, I am not trying to take issue with his position on divorce and remarriage, but I do believe his path for getting to his position was very shaky.

The psalmist states, "Happy are the people whose God is the LORD" (Ps. 144:15). And Romans 14:22 says, "Happy is he who does not condemn himself in what he approves." James writes, "My brethren, take the prophets, who spoke in the name of the Lord, as an example of suffering and patience. Indeed we count them blessed [happy] who endure" (5:10–11).

Many in the current Christian society have tried to create a God who will allow no difficulty or suffering to come into our lives. When I ask for audiences to give me adjectives which will properly describe God, these are the words I hear: *Gracious . . . holy . . . loving . . . sovereign . . . merciful . . . patient . . . kind.*

Did any of these words show up on your list? All of these words truly describe attributes of God. However, did words like *vengeance, jealous,* or *just* appear on your list? Those attributes are all in Scripture, too. Our tendency is to think of God in the context of words such as *kind, faithful, holy, gracious*—all of those sound so comforting, and they fit into our view of God.

Scripture does not teach that He is vengeful, but it teaches He is a God of vengeance (Ps. 94:1). He is the only One who can set the world straight. He is the only One who can balance things out.

In Exodus 34:14 we find, "For the LORD, whose name is Jealous, is a jealous God." I don't ever have someone call that name out when I'm asking for attributes of God.

Jeremiah 51:56 says "For the LORD is the God of recompense / He will surely repay." He will mete out justice. I found the only time we want to consider Him a God of justice is when we hope someone else gets his "just desserts," but we don't want His justice to be applied to us.

When we add all of the characteristics of God together, then we get the full picture of who God is. May I recommend you read *Knowing God by His Names,* by Dick Purnell. This study of the various names given to God in Scripture truly helped me develop a well-rounded picture of God.

When we get the full picture of God—the picture which includes the awesome and the fearsome traits—then we aren't quite so surprised by the things which come into our lives. I have seen, through my experiences of the deaths of three of my children, the compassion God has shown to me and His willingness to interact with me. He has helped me and has been patient with me as I have struggled to learn more about Him and His ways. Jimmy died of crib death when he was seven weeks old in 1964; a year and a half later we had identical twin boys, born on Christmas morning. Ten days later, one of them died. When Ethan died, the second child within a year and a half, I was very angry. I was just plain mad at God. This wasn't fair; I didn't understand it. I asked God, "If You were going to take him away, why did You give me twins in the first place?"

As I stood there and watched that little guy struggle for every breath, I felt God was saying to me, "Marilyn, I loved you enough to die for you. Do you love Me enough to trust Me with this child?" I sat on the floor in the bathroom of the private room the hospital had given us, and I argued with God. After I had spoken my piece, I finally said, "I'm not going to argue anymore. I give You control of this little baby. But just remember, I still don't like it!" I believe God allowed Ethan to live until I could say, "I don't like this, but I'll accept Your will." How thankful I am He knew me well enough to give me some time. I believe my struggle would have been so much harder if I had still been arguing with Him about it when my baby died.

We see in Scripture God even gave Jesus Christ time. When Jesus was faced with His own death, God, in effect, let Him come back and say, "Are You sure? Is that what we have to do? Do we really have to go through that?"

Scripture says, "He went a little farther and fell on His face, and prayed, saying, 'O My Father, if it is possible, let this cup pass from Me: nevertheless not as I will, but as You will'" (Matt. 26:39). In verse 42 of that same chapter, "Again, a second time, He went away" and in verse 44, "So He left them, went away again, and prayed the third time, saying the same words."

I, too, asked God, "Do You know what You're doing? Are You really sure? Isn't there any other way?" But God allowed me to reach the point where I could say, "Okay. Whatever it is, I will accept it. I don't like it, but I'm willing to work with it."

I still had anger and I still had difficulties to work with, but I was not a bitter woman. I am so thankful the bitterness was gone before Ethan died. I was still on speaking terms with God, and He could work with me as we moved along. He gave me time to get to a point where I could agree with Him.

My third child to die was Nathan, seventeen years after his twin brother, Ethan, had died. Nathan was killed by a drunk driver. It was all over before I ever really got to talk to God. The answer was just simply, "No. He's not going to live. He's going to die." You see, this time, I was already at the point where I could say, "I don't understand it, but I trust You."

By the time Nathan died, I had acquired a more balanced picture of God's plan in our lives and a more accurate picture of God Himself. I had learned enough about God to be confident that He had a divine plan, a road map, for me and my family even if I couldn't peek over His shoulder to check it out. I trusted God enough to be able to rest in the belief that Nathan's death was not an "accident" from God's point of view.

I could relate to the psalmist as he said, "I am but a pilgrim here on earth: how I need a map—and your commands are my chart and guide" (Ps. 119:19 TLB).

This statement has been attributed to Charles Spurgeon: "God is too good to be unkind; too wise to be mistaken. . . . When you cannot trace His hand, you can always trust His heart."

I could now gather my understanding of Scripture, the wisdom I had accumulated from godly people, and my personal experience of dealing with God. I could believe that even when I could not trace His hand, I knew I could trust His heart.

To have an effective spiritual life, we have to know Him and trust Him. We have to use what we know through Scripture, through personal experience, and through biblical teaching to get to know God. All of those things together have to work into one whole picture of God. We must use the Bible as our measuring stick to help us create an appropriate picture of Him. Instead, we often want to use our churches, our friends, and our own thoughts as the measuring stick to create a God with whom we can be comfortable.

Now, it isn't wrong to develop individual concepts about God, but we need to make sure they measure up by using Scripture as our yardstick. That is where we will find out, "Is my concept of God right? Is it correct? Does it fit in with what Scripture says?"

As long as we use Scripture as our yardstick, we are on solid ground. Scripture doesn't change. I must tell you, society has changed in the fifty-plus years that I have lived ... a whole lot. But God hasn't changed at all. Scripture has not changed. What was sin fifty years ago is still sin now, according to God—although not according to society and not even according to many churches. But our measuring stick is Scripture, not what's acceptable in our society today.

When Shadrach, Meshach, and Abednego, the Hebrew children who were taken into Babylonian captivity, were being thrown into the fiery furnace, they replied,

> "O Nebuchadnezzar, we have no need to answer you in this matter. If that is the case, our God whom we serve is able to deliver us from the burning fiery furnace, and He will deliver us from your hand, O king. But if not [you see they are giving room for God to be God], let it be known to you, O king, that we do not serve your gods, nor will we worship the gold image which you have set up." (Dan. 3:16–18)

From their point of view, God was still sovereign. He was still the God of Scripture whom they could serve no matter what He chose. Even though they were confident He would save them, they weren't sure if He was going to save them by rescuing them or by taking them home. They just knew He was going to take care of them. But they said, "Even if it doesn't come out the way we think it's going to, we still will serve Him. We will not serve you." And that is where our faith needs to begin. Even if He doesn't do things the way we expect Him to, we will trust Him.

Job states, "Though He slay me, yet will I trust Him" (Job 13:15). You see, it's not, "If He brings all my children back, and everything is wonderful and nothing bad ever happens." It's "Though He slay me, yet will I trust Him." I have faith that no matter who He allows to die, no matter what happens, I can trust that He has the ultimate plan, and He knows what He's doing. Even if I don't have the road map, I am confident He does. And that is knowing and trusting the God of Scripture, the Principal of prayer.

Names of God (NASB)

Names	Characteristics	Key Passage
Advocate	Helper, divine lawyer who pleads our case	1 John 2:1-2
Almighty	All-powerful	Revelation 1:8
Anointed	Messiah	Psalm 2:2
Beloved	Perfectly and uniquely loved by God the Father	Matthew 12:18
Bright Morning Star	Brilliant, awesome	Revelation 22:16
Chosen One	Special to God, anointed	Luke 23:35
Creator	Maker of all	Ecclesiastes 12:1
Deliverer	Rescues, compassionate	Psalm 18:2
Door	Entrance to a relationship with God	John 10:7-9
Eternal Spirit	Equal with the Father and Christ	Hebrews 9:14
Father of Lights	Giver of perfect gifts	James 1:17
Father of Mercies	Kind, sensitive	2 Corinthians 1:3
God Almighty	All-powerful, keeps promises	Genesis 17:1
God of my Salvation	Redeems, rescues	Micah 7:7
God of Recompense	Rewards good or evil	Jeremiah 51:56
God of Vengeance	Just judge, punishes evil	Psalm 94:1
Heavenly Father	Perfect, holy, personal, generous	Luke 11:13
Holy Spirit of God	Righteous third person of the Godhead	Ephesians 4:30
I AM	Eternal LORD	Exodus 3:14
Immanuel	God with us	Matthew 1:23
Jesus Christ	Fully man, fully God	Romans 3:22
Jealous	Righteous zeal	Exodus 34:14
Judge of All	Divine determiner	Hebrews 12:23
King of Glory	Awesome majesty	Psalm 24:7-10
King of Kings	Above all rulers	Revelation 19:16
Lamb of God	God's provision for our sins	John 1:36
Master	Leader, teacher, Lord	2 Peter 2:1
Mediator	Reconciler of God and man	1 Timothy 2:5
Only Begotten Son	Unique, only one of His kind	John 3:16
Only One	Unique relationship with God the Father	Zechariah 14:9
Physician	Divine healer	Luke 4:23
Prince of Life	Author and founder of life	Acts 3:15
Refuge	Gives security, peace	Psalm 46:1
Rock	Security, stable, faithful	Deuteronomy 32:4
Shepherd	Compassionate leader	John 10:11
Spirit of Promise	Seals, gives hope	Ephesians 1:13-14
Teacher	Instructor, communicates truth	Matthew 19:16
Truth	Accurate, reliable, trustworthy	John 14:6
Vine	Source of life and goodness	John 15:1
Vinedresser	Prunes His people to make them bear more fruit	John 15:1
Wonderful Counselor	Totally understands us	Isaiah 9:6
Word of Life	Jesus is God, God's living message	1 John 1:1

Practicing His Presence

1. Look over the names of God above.[1] Which names do you have the most difficulty with? Why?

_____

_____

_____

_____

2. Which names are you most comfortable with? Why?

_____

_____

_____

_____

2

Know His Power

Have you ever considered how consistently the sun comes up each morning and sets each evening? Or how baby animals are born routinely to mother animals who know how to care for them? Or how your words can mysteriously be spoken in the United States and heard in Austrailia all because of a thin little telephone wire? Or have you pondered how God causes a certain verse to appear in your favorite devotional book on a specific day—just when you need it? All of these phenomena are a result of God's power.

Another facet of knowing God is attempting to understand His power. Consider what an angel says to Daniel: "At the beginning of your supplications [as soon as you began to pray] the command went out, and I have come to tell you, for you are greatly beloved; therefore consider the matter, and understand the vision" (9:23). Now that's power: The moment he prayed, the answer was on its way. The God we serve hears us when we pray and He begins to answer immediately.

Deuteronomy 4:7 says, "For what great nation is there that has God so near to it, as the LORD our God is to us, for whatever reason we may call upon Him?" What a privilege to have our Lord God near us when we begin to pray. And He hears us! This is the God we serve.

I have found it is hard for Christians to believe God would allow bad, or what we perceive as bad things, to come into our lives. But once again look at Scripture. The Lord said to Moses, "Who has made man's mouth? Or who makes the mute, the deaf, the seeing, or the blind? Have not I, the LORD?" (Ex. 4:11). Now that is a heavy one, yet this is a side of God we have to accept if we're going to serve Him. He not only gives us good life, or what we call good life, but He allows things to come into our lives that we don't understand and seem negative to us. We don't want to give God responsibility for this area. We want to pass these events off to evil powers. But God says, "I allow those things to happen." All power is owned by Him.

The Old Testament is filled with passages that state things such as, "And the Lord hardened Pharaoh's heart." Now, I don't understand all of these, but it is important for me to know they're there to get a fuller perspective of who it is I love and serve and pray to and worship.

We must study God's Word to get to know Him and to develop a proper perspective on who this Person is. Then when things come into our lives that do not make sense, we are not overwhelmed by them. I remember so often after Nathan died, particularly, it seemed people felt they had to explain God. Nate's death just didn't measure up to what they thought God would do. They didn't think any person should have to bury three children; I agreed with them. But here I was, burying another child. People would come in with explanations, either by projecting about the great and wonderful things that God was going to do, or by explaining God's actions with statements such as, "Well, maybe God knew that Nathan wasn't going to turn out all right so He took him now." Well now, maybe God did know that, but that was not a justification to me for what was happening. You see, what happened was because God is sovereign. And God had made a decision. It was not Satan who had made that decision; it was God. But the only way I knew that was because I was reading Scripture, not because I was listening to everyone around me.

I have come to realize we need to concentrate on who God is, rather than on what He can do. If God is who He says He is, He can do anything He pleases. He has all the power in the world, so we can look to Him to make the right decisions. Then we can concentrate on the fact that He is God, the Creator, the God of all earth. That is Who we serve.

Oswald Chambers puts it in words I can understand.

Prayer alters a man on the inside, alters his mind and his attitude to things. The point of praying is not that we get things from God, but that we learn by prayer to detect the difference between God's order and God's permissive will. God's order is no pain, no sickness, no devil, no war, no sin. His permissive will is all of these things and [I love this term] the soup we are in just now.[1]

Well, we're in the soup, too, just as Chambers was in the soup back in the 1920s. He states, "What a man needs to do is to get hold of God's order in the kingdom on the inside, and then he will begin to see how to handle the riddle of the universe on the outside."[2]

If we have Him in our hearts, if we really know Him, if we are trying to understand His love for us, if we are beginning to comprehend who He is—then we can look at this world and say, "Yes, it's a riddle, but He knows the answer." We won't be disturbed as much that we don't always have the answers because we know the God who does.

Broken Dreams

Lord, look at these broken dreams
    Plans that were not fulfilled.
Each splintered, fractured piece
    Represents hopes that were stilled.

I sift through my pile of plans
    Now just a mound of stubble and tin.
What good are all these pieces?
    Just reminders of what might have been.

You promised beauty for ashes
    And joy after tears,
Perfect peace in the midst of disaster
    And release from all my fears.

Oh, Jesus, please take my burdens.
    I can't carry them anymore.
Help me learn to trust You
    For what life has in store.

Here's my anger, my guilt, my sorrow.
I give You all my pain.
I now release it all to You.
Please let me live again.

M.W.H. 1993

Practicing His Presence

1. What "act of God" has been the most difficult for you to accept?

_____

_____

_____

_____

2. Write a prayer to God and tell Him how you felt when this difficult thing happened. Don't be afraid to speak truthfully. God knows your heart. Nothing is hidden from Him, so there is no reason for you not to speak the truth.

_____

_____

_____

_____

3. Ask God to resolve these issues in your mind. When He does, write it down.

_____

_____

_____

_____

3

Know His Purpose

Have you ever thought of yourself as the praying house of the Son of God? I love this quote:

> The time a Christian gives to prayer and communion with God is not meant for his natural life, but meant to nourish the life of the Son of God in him. God engineers the circumstances of His saints in order that the Spirit may use them as the praying house of the Son of God.[1]

If you have invited Jesus Christ into your life, then the Holy Spirit is offering up prayers in your bodily temple that you know nothing about. The Holy Spirit is making intercession in and through you. Does not that put you in a holy place? It is so humbling to me to think God can use my inner being as a praying house for the Holy Spirit to offer up prayers that I am not even aware of.

God's purpose for prayer first of all is, for all of those He created, to glorify Him. He desires for us to love Him, worship Him, and have fellowship with Him. His purpose is also that He might become known to all men and we might be drawn closer to Him. He wants our eyes to be constantly fixed on Him, eagerly expecting things from Him.

I have a little dog who is a real character. Captain has learned that if he comes near me in the morning when I'm having breakfast, every once in a while I might drop a little crumb for him. Well, instead of just hoping he finds one on the floor, or hoping he happens to be there at the right time, the minute he smells the toast in the toaster, he is next to me. He follows me to the table. He sits right in front of me, following my every move . . . just waiting. His eyes never leave my hand. If I move my hand up, his eyes go up. If I move my hand to the left, his eyes follow my hand. He is watching because I have food for him, and he does not want to miss even one crumb.

That's the way I think we should be with our heavenly Father. Our eyes should be on Him constantly, and we should be eagerly awaiting every morsel. We should let Him see that we are excited about what He might give us and that we understand our food, our joy, our confidence, and our peace all come from Him.

Each time I pray, I create a setting or picture in my mind. Jesus and I may be sitting in my office or some other place in my home, or I may see myself entering His throne room and bowing before Him. Whatever the setting, I focus on His face. I do not see an image I could draw for you, and generally not even an image I could describe in words, but I concentrate on the image He gives me of Himself. First Chronicles says we are to "seek His face evermore" (16:11). I often pray, *Dear Jesus, let me see Your face. Let me sense the response of Your eyes as I talk with You. Keep me sensitive to Your responses that we may always be in tune with each other. In Jesus' Name, Amen.*

One day at a retreat as I prayed with several women, my prayer was similar to the one above. When I finished, a young woman began to pray like this: "Oh, Jesus, thank You for Marilyn's prayer. I have been so impersonal with You; I never even thought of You having eyes. I always thought of You as some nebulous spirit far off from me. Now I realize I can talk to You as I do my closest friend and we can respond to each other."

Psalm 32:8 says, "I will guide you with My eye." Have you ever watched a parent "guide" a child with his eye? My children knew exactly where they stood with me simply by watching my eyes. Approval or disapproval can be communicated instantly through the look in a person's eye. Right now, can you sense how Jesus is looking at you? Is he conveying pride, approval, frustration, sadness? It is possible to have such a close relationship with Him that you can be guided by His eye.

If you have a poor relationship with your parents, or if you have been victimized by the father-figure in your life, you may have difficulty relating to God as Father. If you have not had a human model you can comfortably equate to a heavenly father, I would like to suggest that you look over some of the names of God that are listed on page 8.

On a journal page, start your prayer with a different name for God than you have ever used before and build a setting around that name. One of the names I have enjoyed using is "O King, O Sovereign King." In Scripture David said many times, "My King and my Lord." In Deuteronomy He is referred to as "Our Sovereign Lord." When I think "king," I think of myself entering the royal palace, walking in, and bowing before my king. Then I see myself able to tell Him the things that I need because He has summoned me to come into His presence.

This kind of exercise can refresh our prayer life and add some excitement to it that maybe we haven't had in quite a while. Choose a name or names that appeal to you which will cause you to worship and glorify God. Write your prayer to God using these new names. Picture yourself in each new setting and share your thoughts with God.

Speak, My Lord

Speak, my Lord,
Thy servant hears.
Please, oh King,
Banish my fears.

Open my eyes
To see Thy face.
Let me rejoice
In Your embrace.

I feel Your touch.
You are with me now.
I am Your servant.
Before You I bow.

M.W.H. 1992

Practicing His Presence

1. Write your prayer using a different name for God than you have ever used before, one that emphasizes how deserving He is to receive our glory and worship. Draw a verbal picture of the setting.

Eternal and most holy Father in Heaven: I lift my prayer to You. I see You sitting upon a glowing, golden throne. Your white robes glow and your face is radient with Compassion, Strength & love.

4

Know His Protection

When I was young, I remember hearing pastors and missionaries talk about Satan, demonic activity, and spiritual warfare. However, I got the distinct impression that Christians didn't really have to be too concerned about Satan and satanic attacks unless they were missionaries in a foreign land! It was not popular to talk about such things in America. Surely we were safe from such things. While we were all patting ourselves on the back and feeling very comfortable, Satan was quietly moving in and quickly possessing the land.

It is impossible to live an effective Christian life today without acknowledging we are in constant spiritual warfare. "Be sober, be vigilant; because your adversary the devil walks about like a roaring lion, seeking whom he may devour" (1 Peter 5:8).

Satan will not always be easy to recognize. He does not run around in a red suit with horns, a tail, and a pitchfork. The apostle Paul warns "For Satan himself transforms himself into an angel of light" (2 Cor. 11:14).

Where will we be likely to find those who appear to be angels of light, those who are trying to trip us up? Most probably they are right in our churches among the genuine Christians. The Church definitely has its counterfeits. Satan is much more concerned about what is going on with Christians than what's going on in the red light or drug districts of our cities. Satan has already captured many of the people there, but he doesn't have us. He is acutely interested in what's going on in the Christian community, but we have the power to hold him off.

Charles Spurgeon stated, "[Satan] can make men dance upon the brink of hell as though they were on the verge of heaven."[1] I think many of us are doing that today. We are living on the edge, letting Satan tempt us with worldly ways, while still trying to identify with the Christian community. We do not recognize the danger we are putting ourselves in.

James encourages, "Therefore submit to God. Resist the devil and he will flee from you" (4:7).

God has warned us about Satan, but He has also given us the power to win the battles that come our way. We must access the power He has given us if we want to really experience the victorious Christian life that Christ has promised us.

Paul tells us to "put on the whole armor of God, that you may be able to stand against the wiles of the devil" (Eph. 6:11).

This past year I was invited to a secular event to share the story of the deaths of my three children with a group of bereaved parents. After I agreed to go, I discovered that the main speaker for the day was a noted leader in the New Age movement in our area. As we were driving to the event, I began to feel panicked. I started chiding myself: *What in the world are you doing speaking on the same platform with a New Ager? You'll be eaten alive!*

As my husband, Glen, drove, I began to pray outloud:

Dear Jesus, Your Word says, "He who is in you is greater than he who is in the world" (1 John 4:4). Right now I feel scared, but I am asking that You will show Your greatness through me today. Give me courage and give me strength.

Lord, I also ask if this man intends to share untruth with these people today, please confuse his thoughts and his words. Protect this audience from hearing false teachings. Thank You for what You are going to do. In Jesus' Name, Amen.

My part of the meeting went very well, and then the New Ager began to speak. Even though I was not anxious to hear his propaganda, I was curious to watch his style of presentation because I had heard how dynamic and impressive he was as a speaker.

As he began to speak, it seemed he was just rambling. I wondered when he was going to start to be impressive and dynamic. After a few minutes, he stopped, looked at his notes, turned the pages over a few times and then said, "Now what did I plan to share today?" He struggled for a few more minutes and finally said, "I guess I'll open it up for questions."

It was a little hard for people to come up with questions since he hadn't really said much, but finally one member of the audience asked him a question. After the speaker answered the question, the listener commented, "I've already tried that, but it didn't work."

After two or three more futile attempts to answer questions, the speaker said, "Well, I guess it's time for lunch."

As I walked out in absolute awe of what the Lord had done, a woman came up to me and said, "Honey, you're a hard act to follow!" I chuckled to myself as the Lord reminded me once again, "Greater is He that is in you than he that is in the world." That day the score for the battle was *God 1, Satan 0.* I wonder how often it has been the other way around, *God 0, Satan 1,* because we haven't realized that the power to win the battle is constantly with us. All we have to do is utilize the power we already have. "The God of peace will crush Satan under your feet shortly" (Rom. 16:20).

Jesus gave us a very clear example of how to resist the devil through his forty days in the wilderness. Each time Satan confronted Jesus, Jesus answered him with Scripture. Scripture is to be a major part of our armor. If we have God's Word in our heart and mind, we will always have ammunition to thwart Satan's attempts to confuse and conquer us.

Oswald Chambers says, "The very powers of darkness are paralyzed by prayer. No wonder Satan tries to keep our minds fuzzy in active work, so we cannot think to pray."[2]

Satan understands the power of prayer a whole lot better than we do. I jokingly and yet almost seriously said to someone recently "I am so busy working on this book on prayer, I hardly have time to pray."

And that can happen. Satan would love to so preoccupy me with the mechanics of prayer that I might forget to pray.

I have also had more than the average share of difficulties and irritating interruptions in the last few weeks since I was preparing this manuscript than I've probably had in the last year. Some of them have been good and some not so good, but they have all been deterrents to the flow of my writing.

On the morning that I began this chapter, I planned to dedicate the entire day to writing. As Glen walked out the door for work, he noticed water running across our front sidewalk. A quick investigation showed that the pipe connecting our house to the city water supply had ruptured. So before Glen went to work, he waited for the plumber to find out what the financial damage was going to be. Then he left me as I tried to concentrate on my writing while the plumber dug up our front lawn. A little later my parents called and asked if they could stop by for a few minutes. Then a friend called, trying to find my parents. When he realized they were coming to my house, he decided to stop by my house to visit with them. Of course I felt I should offer them all a cup of coffee, and thus went the morning. I had to try to resume my writing in what was left of the afternoon.

As I remembered Chambers's statement, "The very powers of darkness are paralyzed by prayer," I began to realize Satan would be working very hard to keep me from encouraging fellow Christians to pray. And I thought about this also: "Satan tries to keep our minds fuzzy in active work, so we cannot think to pray." So that's what we have to be on guard for. When you determine to learn to pray effectively, you are going to have interruptions. Satan will try to distract you any way he can, *even with good things*.

While Scripture teaches very clearly that Satan is a defeated foe, it also teaches we are not to regard his attacks lightly. In Jude 9 we read, "Yet Michael the archangel, in contending with the devil, when he disputed about the body of Moses, dared not bring against him a reviling accusation, but said, 'The Lord rebuke you!'"

We need to be careful not to be in conversation with Satan or become preoccupied with his plans and his presence. I have found the most comfortable way for me to address an obvious satanic attack is to simply say, "Satan, in the Name of Jesus, be gone," or better yet to say, "The Lord rebuke you! Be gone." Then I just go on with the assignment God has given me and let Him take care of Satan.

We must be careful to always practice the presence of Jesus and not the presence of Satan. Keep your eyes on Jesus.

Practicing His Presence

1. Think of times that Satan has defeated you. How did he do it? Did he use another person? Did he use an emotion such as fear, anger, or guilt? Looking back, how could you have resisted his attack? Look up some Bible verses that would have helped you.

_____

_____

_____

_____

2. As you write your prayer, talk to Jesus about the areas where you are vulnerable to Satan's attack. Ask Jesus to show you ways of escape.

_____

_____

_____

_____

5

Know His Presence

We are living in a day when most Christians are afraid of the supernatural. In many ways this is understandable considering all of the hype we have been exposed to through Hollywood via movies and television. We have also heard and seen bizarre happenings through those who are involved in the New Age, occultic practices, and satanism.

Many Christians realize that, while some of the things we hear and see through the cults may well be real, the power source is Satan rather than God. Since most of us find it rather scary to think too long about Satan, many in the Christian world have simply decided to throw out all supernatural, assuming it is all satanic. When we do that, Christianity itself becomes more a pared-down, mechanical routine than an exciting, beyond-our-understanding kind of experience. Today, however, it seems if we can't explain it, we negate it.

Thank goodness King David, Daniel, Isaiah, Peter, Paul, and the other writers of the Old and New Testaments were not afraid of the supernatural. They had cults and imitations in their day, too, but rather than "throwing the baby out with the bath water," they simply learned to recognize the authentic. We must do the same.

Without imagination, the Christian life becomes bland and sterile. When I mention the cross, each of you will immediately have a picture in your mind of a cross. For some it will be the beautiful cross hung at the front of their church, for others, it will be an image of a roughly hewn cross put together with split logs. The descriptions could go on and on because God works individually and uniquely with each of us in a way that will speak to us. But the point is this: We will all have some image in our minds. God made us that way, and when Christ walked this earth, He capitalized on the picture-making faculty of human beings.

Christ spoke in verbal pictures, called parables, throughout His ministry. It is sometimes hard for us to separate the parables and the actual happenings in the Bible because we have had to draw verbal and mental pictures of both types of events. I believe that is okay because God wanted us to learn from both the parables, such as the prodigal son and the good Samaritan, and the actual events, such as the raising of Lazarus and Peter's walking on the water.

The Lord gave us all of our creative ability and He didn't expect us to ignore it; He just asks that we employ it in righteous directions. One word the Christian world has become very afraid of in the recent past is *imagination*. Since the New Age began to use words such as *imagine* and *visualize*, the Christians have stopped using those words. What nonsense! A human being would be extremely crippled without his ability to imagine. God the Father created our imagination and gave us the word *imagination* long before the New Agers ever thought of it. Instead of avoiding the word, we need to take it back and claim it for Jesus.

Isaiah 26:3 states, "You will keep him in perfect peace, whose mind is stayed on You." Some translations of Scripture exchange "mind" and "imagination" in this verse so that it says "Thou wilt keep him in perfect peace whose imagination is stayed on Thee."

Oswald Chambers asks:

Is your imagination stayed on God or is it starved? The starvation of the imagination is one of the most fruitful sources of exhaustion and sapping in a worker's life. If you have never used your imagination to put yourself before God, begin to do it now. It is no use waiting for

God to come; you must put your imagination away from the face of idols and look unto Him and be saved. Imagination is the greatest gift God has given us and it ought to be devoted entirely to Him. If you have been bringing every thought into captivity to the obedience of Christ, it will be one of the greatest assets to faith when the time of trial comes, because your faith and the Spirit of God will work together. Learn to associate ideas worthy of God with all that happens in Nature—the sunrises and the sunsets, the sun and the stars, the changing seasons, and your imagination will never be at the mercy of your impulses, but will always be at the service of God.[1]

Let me give you some examples of how we can utilize our imagination in getting to know God better.

I am the good shepherd; and I know My sheep, and am known by My own. (John 10:14)

I will never leave you nor forsake you. (Heb. 13:5)

The angel of the LORD encamps all around those who fear Him,
And delivers them. (Ps. 34:7)

What do those verses mean to you? What pictures do they bring to your mind?

For me, I see Jesus always with me. I don't think of Him just dwelling in my heart; He is *with* me. He walks beside me. He takes my hand and leads me. He listens as I speak. He sits in the front row and encourages me as I speak. His eyes sadden when I fail Him and brighten when I please Him just as a father's should.

As the Good Shepherd I see Him holding me, stroking my head, and protecting me just as a shepherd would care for his sheep.

I have also become more conscious of the work of angels in God's structure of things. I often ask for Him to draw His angels close in around me to protect me and minister to me when I am speaking. I have never consciously seen an angel, but there are many times when I am aware of their presence.

Recently I read *The Journals of Jim Elliot,* one of the missionaries murdered by Auca Indians in Ecuador in 1956. He had some interesting thoughts about angels.

> But a phrase in A. C.'s [Amy Carmichael's] Gold Cord struck me as I read this evening. Speaking of men in the Services of India who helped in the work of rescuing children from the temples she says (p. 137) "... being known to be on the side of the angels." I must consider this strongly. Carelessly, I suppose, I have left these ministering spirits to themselves. But Peter warned me this morning that I had obtained a salvation into which angels desired to look [1 Peter 1:12]. There must be more care about my talk on their account, since they are to be instructed by me. I must develop an awareness of them and see them work, since one day I must judge them. I must learn reverence before them (women wear hats for angels' sake [allusion to 1 Cor. 11:10]); they know my God's holiness better than I. So we shall teach one another, my spirit friends. We are both servants of God, both His creatures, and we must learn cooperation. May I be found worthy of this compact that I make with you tonight, comrades angelical. Let us together honor God, to whom be dominion, the right and power to reign, both now and forevermore. Amen.[2]

Chambers says we should "live facing Jesus."[3] Those three words have been rolling around in my head for over a year now.

How would you live facing Jesus? Recently Glen and I spent a week in Bermuda where I spoke at a women's seminar. One afternoon on a tour of the island, the tour guide stopped at a special view point. We had to climb a steep, craggy hill. Glen went ahead of me with his arm thrust backward so that I could hang on to him and follow in his footsteps. I was totally absorbed in watching his feet. As Glen moved his foot forward, I would place my foot where his had been. When we got to the top, I looked around to see a most glorious view of the ocean, but then I realized if I hadn't been so busy watching Glen's feet, I would have been able to see this same view most of the way up the mountain. Many of us spend our time following Jesus, footstep after plodding footstep, and we miss the view on the trip.

In contrast to following Jesus, as I live facing Jesus, with the eyes of my heart, I see Jesus standing in front of me. Sometimes He is holding my hand, walking backward because He knows where He is going. The path is familiar to Him. I fix my eyes on Him and He gently leads my every move. Now I hope you won't flinch too much, but I see my walk with Jesus as a dance. He leads, and I simply follow His leading. We can chat together along the way. Sometimes we can shut the rest of the world out and simply move in our own little world. Often our steps are short and quick, other times they are very broad, but He never lets go of me. Just as it was with Peter when he walked on the water, I'm safe just as long as I keep my eyes on Jesus.

The writer of Hebrews reminds us there is "so great a cloud of witnesses" (12:1) sitting in the heavenly grandstands cheering us on as we run the race of life. I give a message frequently entitled "What Trips You Up?" In this message I have several women from the seminar read scripts I have prepared of women from the Bible speaking to my audience. I include Sarah, Rebekah, Mary, Martha, and other Bible women.

One day as I was sitting in the front row of a church getting ready to give that message, God let my imagination draw a picture for me. I saw Jesus sitting on a throne and several women were gathered around the throne. I heard them say, "Listen. . . . She's going to start talking about us really soon!"

I had to chuckle at my picture, but I also took time to thank Jesus that He had let His Word become real in my mind. All through that message I thought of those women about whom I was speaking. They aren't some fictitious characters in an obsolete book. They are real; they are alive with Jesus; and I believe they are cheering me on.

Is the Word alive to you? Is Jesus alive to you? Ask God to allow your righteous imagination to become active in a way that will give you some excitement in your Christian walk. Keep your imagination stayed on Him and let His Word come alive in your life.

Practicing His Presence

1. In your prayer time today, ask God to allow your imagination
    to become righteously active. What picture do you get when
    you think of living "facing Jesus"? Write down your thoughts
    about "facing Jesus" and also the other verses I shared in
    this chapter.

    I feel a warm sense of Jesus'
    being near me. I see in my
    closed eyes a deep magenta light
    that I know represents Jesus'
    presence.

2. As you pray, place yourself before the heavenly Father.
    Create a setting. See yourself talking with Him. Draw a verbal
    picture as you pray facing Jesus. Practice His presence today.

    _____

    _____

    _____

    _____

Part

2

THE PROBLEMS OF PRAYER

6

Distractions

Last year, on a Sunday evening, I arrived home from a week-long trip to Georgia. I left for Georgia on December 1 and when I arrived home a week later I was immediately into the throes of Christmas. My husband was into his second week of performances in a church-sponsored Christmas pageant. Because of his busy schedule he had caught a bad cold, so each day he was going into work for a while, coming home and resting, and then going out to the church each evening. Each year while he performs in this Christmas event, I try to have several dinner parties after which I take our guests out to enjoy the Christmas pageant. My week's schedule included a dinner party on Tuesday night, a dinner at church on Wednesday evening, picking my parents up at the train station on Friday and giving a dinner party Friday night, not to mention a hair appointment, a nail appointment, a doctor's appointment, and making sure someone was at the house on Wednesday afternoon when my new couch was to be delivered. And just to throw a little excitement into my uneventful week, I received notice that I was to appear for jury duty on Thursday morning!

On Monday morning Glen and I managed a few minutes to pray together before he left for work and I left for my doctor's appointment. Tuesday morning I spent a short time with the Lord and rushed off to my hair appointment while Glen slept in for a little while. Wednesday I hurried off to the church prayer meeting at 7:00 A.M. but I didn't get my own private time with the Lord until much later in the day. Thursday, I overslept and awoke with less than an hour remaining before I had to report for jury duty. Needless to say, I had no quiet time at home, but the Lord did talk to me while I was driving in to the city. He talked to me regarding my poor attitude about serving on a jury! It took Him most of the trip to get me to change my attitude, so I had little time to talk with Him; I mostly listened. My time had to come later in the day. So I sat in the jury room writing this chapter and reflecting on my week while I was waiting to see if I would be assigned to a particular case.

I have given you this little scenario of a typical week in my life to emphasize one of the reasons we don't pray: We think we don't have time, and we allow other things to distract us. Most certainly this generation is generally in a time pressure cooker—which is all the more reason why we *must* pray.

Martin Luther stated: "I have so much to do today that I shall never get through it with less than three hours' prayer."[1] Charles Spurgeon commented, "I always feel that there is something wrong if I go without prayer for even half an hour in the day."[2]

Even before we put a foot out of our bed, we should practice saying "Good morning, Lord." It is so important to start the day by acknowledging His presence in our lives and in our hearts, and continue that practice all day long.

As the psalmist wrote: "It is good to say, 'Thank you' to the Lord, to sing praises to the God who is above all gods. Every morning tell him, 'Thank you for your kindness,' and every evening rejoice in all his faithfulness" (Ps. 92:1-2 TLB).

I do not believe it is my place to put manmade rules and standards of performance on anyone except myself. Therefore I do not intend to impose specific standards on you such as "You must have a lengthy quiet time every day"; "You must read the Bible through each year"; or "You must write your prayers."

While I do many of these things because I enjoy doing them, I find if I set specific constraints for myself in these areas, it is easy to become legalistic and prideful. It is possible for those of us who do have a consistent, organized prayer life to become very judgmental of those who do not, and at times we can even question the spirituality of one who is not following in our specific pattern.

However, I do believe it is easier for me to walk a desirable Christian life when I am consistent in having a quiet time. But I have also observed it is easy for us to have faith in our prayer life rather than faith in the *God* of our prayer life, the Principal of prayer. So I try very hard not to judge others just because I may pray longer than they do each day. I also try not to judge *me* if I miss a day in my quiet time. But I know my spiritual life goes downhill very quickly if I do not spend time with the Lord each day, so I have a strong desire to communicate with Him on a regular basis.

Some days, as in the week I described for you, it seems the Lord and I are talking on the run, but we're talking. The entry in my prayer journal may be very short. Other times I feel as if I could write all day long, and frequently I do write in my journal for more than an hour. Then it is because the Lord and I have so much to say to each other that day, not that I am requiring it of myself.

So don't force your time with the Lord. Do determine that you will at least say "Good morning, Lord" each day and that you will seek to hear Him say "Good morning, my child" back to you so that the dialogue has begun. My friend Linda is beginning the discipline of listening to God. She told me that she sets aside seven minutes a day to be completely quiet as she listens for His voice. That may not sound like much time, but it is my belief that Linda's seven minutes will soon stretch into a longer period of time. As she gets excited about hearing God speak to her, she will desire to spend more time with Him. It should be our desire to spend as much time as possible with Jesus each day, and our lives should be a running commentary of conversation with Him. I encourage you to set some realistic goals for yourself. Plan to read and study God's Word and have a good prayer time each day. But if it doesn't always work out that way, don't feel guilty. Work on doing better, but don't let Satan discourage you so much that you stop trying to pray.

A few years ago in December, my daughter-in-law's father—my grandchildren call him "Papa"—had a stroke. The entire family was in shock since he was just in his late forties. We all tried to rally around to help Debbie with the children so she could spend time with her father at the hospital.

One day I took the children, two-year-old Nathan and four-year-old Kate, to the mall. I saw a shop where the children could have their pictures taken and embossed on a cup. I thought that would be a great gift for Papa since he was not able to see the children often. I checked with a clerk and found we would have to wait forty-five minutes to have their pictures taken. To this grandma, forty-five minutes seemed like a long time to walk around a mall with two children under the age of five. So I told Kate we would have to try later, after we went to my parents' house for lunch.

After lunch, on the way back to our house, I told Kate I was afraid Nathan would be asleep by the time we got to the mall and suggested we buy something else for Papa later. Kate started to cry and said, "I think Papa needs our picture."

Well, of course, Grammie couldn't handle her tears, so I said, "Kate, we need to pray that Nate won't fall asleep before we get to the mall and that there won't be a long waiting line." Almost before I got the words out of my mouth, I heard this sweet little voice coming from the back seat, *Dear Jesus, we really need to buy that cup for Papa. Please help Nathan to stay awake and help there be no line at the picture place. Thank You. Amen.*

The faith of a little child! She didn't have to wait for the perfect time or the perfect place to pray. She had an urgent need and she prayed immediately. When we got to the mall Nathan was wide awake, and we didn't have to wait. The picture turned out to be beautiful, but I got the best present when I heard my granddaughter pray. After all, "a little child shall lead them" (Isa. 11:6).

Chambers reinforces what I learned from Kate. "There is always a suitable place to pray, to lift up your eyes to God; there is no need to get to a place of prayer, pray wherever you are."[3]

Practicing His Presence

1. Describe the kind of quiet prayer time you want to have with God and how often you want to have it.

_____

_____

_____

_____

2. If you do not have that right now, what is keeping you from it?

_____

_____

_____

_____

3. What would you have to do to change the situation?

_____

_____

_____

_____

4. Are you willing to do the things you stated above to start having the kind of prayer time you want to have with the Lord?

_____

_____

_____

_____

5. Please write a short letter to the Lord telling Him why you have not spent more time with Him and what you are going to do to change the situation. Then sign and date your prayer as evidence of your commitment.

_____

_____

_____

_____

_____

_____

_____

_____   _____

NAME   DATE

7

Disappointment

Recently I shared my concern with some women about how few Christians spend even five minutes a day in prayer. I stated, "It is obvious that in my book I need to teach people how to pray."

Then one of the women commented, "I know how to pray. I used to have a very effective prayer life, but I don't anymore."

I asked, "When did your prayer life change?"

"When I got married. I always hoped I would be able to have a regular prayer time with the man I married. We did at first, but then it dropped off. Now, when I suggest we pray together, he says I'm nagging him. Once our prayer time stopped, my own prayer time began to lag also. Now I'm angry at my husband, and I guess I'm mad at God, too."

I have met very few couples who have consistently had a good mutual prayer time throughout their marriage. Glen and I prayed a little together before we were married and tried to establish a pattern after we were married of praying each evening as we went to bed. Actually, in our early prayer times, Glen prayed and I listened. I found it very hard to listen intently that late at night when I had so little participation, so often I fell asleep before Glen ended his prayer. That was very irritating to him, and our attempt to pray together ended quite quickly.

Over the years we have occasionally made sincere, though futile, attempts to reestablish a mutual prayer time. However, two years ago while on a cruise, we participated in a marriage seminar where we were gently nudged into confronting each other regarding the reasons we didn't pray together. I shared that I felt I was an onlooker while Glen prayed. He admitted he felt my disinterest keenly.

Glen and I have come a long way since our early years of marriage. He is not as threatened by my ability to express myself clearly and converse with little hesitation. Now he seldom looks at these abilities as a threat to his role as head of the house. I have learned to appreciate his thoughtful, more reticent speech patterns. I am learning to listen and seek out his logic rather than see each lull in his conversation as an opportunity for me to jump in and "liven things up."

So this time as we once again attempted to pray together, it worked. We agreed that Glen would get up early enough in the morning for us to have time to pray together before he left for work. One day he prays, and the next day I pray. Besides praying together, we also use this time to just talk over the upcoming events of the day. Now I know what meetings Glen will have each day, and he knows what I have scheduled. How I love the days when he prays and I hear him pray for me and my ministry and he tells the Lord how much he loves me and how proud he is of me.

I know he enjoys the days that I pray for him and his work. I often pray that he will not just see the men as employees, but he will see them as people who need his gentle approach and understanding.

Don't give up on your hope of a good prayer time with your partner or your family, but don't let disappointment in another person keep you from nurturing your own prayer life.

Perhaps rather than a marriage situation, a trauma has occurred in your life which brought great disappointment, possibly with yourself as well as with God. When my sons died, my heart was so sick I could not pray even though I had a very consistent prayer life and quiet time prior to their deaths. The longest sentence I could utter was "Lord, help me." Trauma causes us to be unable to concentrate on any one thing longer than a few seconds, and that inability to focus enters into our spiritual life as well as our physical life.

However, I also realize I was disappointed with God. I remember a close family member who stated repeatedly after Nate's death, "I never thought God would do this." While I didn't say those words aloud, I certainly agreed with the thought, "I never thought God would do this." When I tried to pray, a multitude of emotions so overwhelmed me, I could not pray. No words would come.

Now my particular approach was to keep trying until I was able to read a full sentence from the Bible and understand it and until I was able to utter at least a few words in prayer before I melted into a puddle of tears. Yet for some, the disappointment they feel within themselves toward God has become a barrier between them and God and they have quit trying to pray.

Can you relate to that? Are you disappointed with God? Perhaps you need to do as the psalmist did and admit your disappointment with God. He can handle it, and He wants to hear from you!

Before you take time to write in your journal today listen to some of the statements from the Psalms. I know I can often identify with these and I'm sure you can, too.

I cry to the Lord; I call and call to him. Oh, that he would listen. I am in deep trouble and I need his help so badly. All night long I pray, lifting my hands to heaven, pleading. There can be no joy for me until he acts. I think of God and moan, overwhelmed with longing for his help. I cannot sleep until you act. I am too distressed even to pray! (Ps. 77:1-4 TLB)

We live within the shadow of the Almighty, sheltered by the God who is above all gods. This I declare, that he alone is my refuge, my place of safety; he is my God, and I am trusting him. (Ps. 91:1-2 TLB)

In my distress I prayed to the Lord and he answered me and rescued me. He is for me! How can I be afraid? What can mere man do to me? The Lord is on my side, he will help me. (Ps. 118:5-7 TLB)

I am completely discouraged—I lie in the dust. Revive me by your Word. (Ps. 119:25 TLB)

I weep with grief; my heart is heavy with sorrow; encourage and cheer me with your words. (Ps. 119:28 TLB)

O Lord, listen to my prayers; give me the common sense you promised. Hear my prayers; rescue me as you said you would. I praise you for letting me learn your laws. I will sing about their wonder, for each of them is just. Stand ready to help me because I have chosen to follow your will. (Ps. 119:169–173 TLB)

King David was not afraid to share his frustration and discouragement. Rather than become silent before God, he told the Lord just how he felt. I encourage you to do the same thing. If you're disappointed with God, if you're frustrated, if you're discouraged—say so. He wants to talk with you.

Practicing His Presence

1. Reread the Psalms in this chapter. If these don't express your thoughts, then thumb through the book of Psalms until you find some statements that come close to how you feel right now. Write down those Psalms.

_____

_____

_____

_____

2. Now tell the Lord how you are feeling. He wants to hear from you regardless of how you feel about Him. Be honest as you share your thoughts with Him today.

_____

_____

_____

_____

8

Disconnection

Have you ever felt disconnected from God? Perhaps it was because of some trouble that you were facing, or perhaps you felt distant because of something you had done. The psalmist could relate to our feelings when he said, "If you, LORD, should mark iniquities, O LORD, who could stand? But there is forgiveness with You, that You may be feared" (Ps. 130:3-4).

On a recent trip, I stayed several days in the same hotel. One particular bellhop seemed to be on call each time I needed my books carted down to the front door. Joe was a very friendly young man and always seemed happy to help me. His gentle spirit seemed to belie his burly appearance which was aided by his long, shaggy hair and his tatoo-laden arms.

The day I left, as he set my baggage in the lobby, I thanked him and gave him a copy of my book *When Your Dreams Die*. Joe knelt down beside my chair and very quietly asked, "Can God be mad at you?"

I asked, "Do you feel God is mad at you right now?"

Joe nodded. "I've done some bad things, and now everything is going wrong in my life. God must be mad at me."

Joe presented a very strong reason why many of us quit praying: unconfessed sin puts distance between us and God. God is not mad at us; it's more that we're mad at ourselves and assume He must be, too. We're going in the wrong direction and we don't know how to get turned around.

Years ago I heard Dr. Henry Brandt describe knowing he was going in the wrong direction on the freeway, but he kept going that way because he couldn't figure out how he could get turned around without admitting to his wife and other passengers in the car that he had been going the wrong way.

Many times we are like that: We keep trying to figure out a way to change directions without admitting we have gone the wrong way. Confession of sin is seldom easy but it is vital to our walk with the Lord.

Recently, I came home from a short trip and routinely checked my answering machine. The voice on one message was that of a young man perhaps in his early twenties. He said, "Hi, this is Peter. I'm trying to reach Cheryl. I think this used to be her number, but I'm not sure if it is now or not. I just wanted to tell Cheryl that I'm sorry for the way I treated her in high school, and I hope she'll forgive me."

Bless his heart! How I wish I'd been home to take that message. Peter needed someone to hear his confession. He needed to be heard so badly he confessed to an answering machine!

In the past few years, I have begun to understand the value of the confessional. Not that we necessarily need to confess to a priest or a minister, but James 5:16 states, "Confess your trespasses to one another, and pray for one another, that you may be healed."

When I was a little girl, it was not uncommon for people to walk forward at the end of a church service to confess sin and pray with the pastor or a prayer counselor. While only God can cleanse us of our sins, being willing to confess our sin to another human being is very healthy. Not that we should broadcast our sins to the world, but admitting to someone else the areas where we are struggling to live the Christian life is important. In the Christian community, however, we have moved away from any kind of public accountability. Because of this we seldom become aware of how even a close friend struggles against sin until he loses the battle and his sin becomes public.

A few years ago I attended a week-long prayer and emotional healing seminar. On the second day, the leader announced she felt

God was telling her she should not continue with the seminar until there was confession of sin among those who were in attendance.

First, I was absolutely amazed at her forthrightness, but then I thought, *Well, we'll all bow our heads, pray and confess our sins privately, and then we can get on with this seminar.*

You can imagine my shock when the leader said, "I want everyone to whom God is speaking to please stand. Then I want you to come down here where my team is waiting. Speak with one of them, confess your sin to them; then the two of you can take your sin to the Father, place it at the cross, and proclaim it forgiven."

I thought, *No one will do that. It's too embarrassing.* Then I looked up and realized over two hundred people were making their way to the front of the church!

Recently I conducted a seminar attended by over four hundred women. At the end of the day, I made a similar invitation. I was a little nervous since I had never given an open invitation before, but I felt very strongly that God knew that some people in the audience needed to have someone else hear their confession of a particular sin or that they needed to state their declaration of forgiveness toward a particular individual. During the last song, I stood near the front and was thrilled when three women came forward. While the rest of the audience was leaving, I was absorbed in praying individually with these three women. When I concluded with them, I assumed my counseling time was over, but as I looked up, I saw a sea of faces looking at me.

I innocently asked, "Are you waiting for me to sign books?"

One of the ladies in the front of the group said, "No, we're here to confess!"

I spent the next two and a half hours praying with each lady and hearing her confession. We then prayed together and placed her sin and her repentance at the cross and thanked God for the cleansing and freedom He is waiting to give us when we confess our sins.

A young woman with whom I have prayed off and on for several years came to talk to me recently. Her basic comment was, "I have tried everything you have suggested, but things still are not going well in my family. Even though I spend quite a bit of time in prayer and Bible study, my efforts to improve my relationship with my husband and children seem to be fruitless. I feel I am fighting an enemy I can't see."

I questioned her thoroughly regarding her own spiritual walk. I asked if there were any hidden, unconfessed sins, any addictions, any secrets. Since I had also counseled her and her husband jointly about their family problems, I felt her answer was very sincere when she said "No, I've told you everything."

After she spoke, I sat quietly while God spoke to me, and then I said, "If you have really tried all of the things I have suggested and you still feel defeated, and if there truly is no hidden sin in your own life, I want you to very gently talk with your husband when you get home and ask him the same questions I just asked you. You can tell him Marilyn feels very strongly there is some hidden sin in the camp."

Well, I've never done anything like that before, and it will probably be a long time before I do it again, but I believed very strongly God was leading me in my words. After the young woman went home, I prayed fervently. Within an hour I had a phone call from the young husband. When he came over, he admitted that there was a hidden sin, and that he couldn't loose himself of this addiction. We spent a lot of time in prayer and confession that afternoon, and then he went home to talk with his wife. Life will not immediately be all sweetness and light for this couple, but Satan no longer has a stronghold, and they no longer feel they are disconnected from God. Jesus will see them through this major difficulty.

We are a hurting, sinful people, in need of a Savior, but we also need a body of flesh and bones to whom we can admit our sins and our struggles, a fellow struggler to whom we can be accountable.

Practicing His Presence

1. As I read this chapter, God spoke to me about the following sin(s):

   _____

   _____

   _____

   _____

2. For each one pray this prayer:

   Father, I confess the sin of _____ to You. I repent of this sin and ask You to forgive me and cleanse me.

3. Ask God whether you need to confess this sin to another person. If so, write down the name of that person in the space below. As soon as possible go to this person and pray the above prayer in his or her presence.

   _____

   Then have that person pray:

   Father, I have heard the prayer of _____ as he confessed the sin of _____ . Your Word stated in 1 John 1:9: "If we confess our sins, He is faithful and just to forgive us our sins and to cleanse us from all unrighteousness." Therefore, Father, as _____ has confessed and repented of this sin, in the name of Jesus we proclaim him cleansed and forgiven. Thank You, Jesus. Amen.

9

Disinformation

My husband tells me "disinformation" is a new buzzword in the business world. It refers to willfully spreading biased or erroneous information as truth, and it fits a situation I repeatedly see in the Christian arena.

Often as Christians we look to our churches and our colleagues to build our theology rather than basing our doctrinal stand on what God's Word says. When God doesn't perform according to our theology, we become disenchanted with Christianity and with God Himself. Often we stop praying because we have based our prayer life on disinformation.

I do not intend to discuss or disprove certain theories, but let me merely list some areas of disinformation that confuse us and keep us from praying. Because of these, we may have lost faith in God by putting faith in disinformation.

Bad things don't happen to good people.
If I had enough faith, my prayers would be answered.
Christians shouldn't grieve.
Only those who speak in tongues are really spiritual.
Speaking in tongues is of the devil and not of God.
If anyone dies before the age of seventy, it is because of sin in his or
    her life.

God wants all Christians to be wealthy.

God wants all Christians to be healthy.

I am not good enough, so God won't listen to me.

If I try to pray, God will discover how little faith I have.

If I pray, God is going to require me to do something too difficult, something I don't want to do.

Christians should never be angry at God or question Him.

God is sovereign so it doesn't matter if I pray or not.

I know you could add many other statements to this list, and at the end of this chapter I will suggest you do just that.

Rather than my taking time to refute the above statements, let me simply say I believe Scripture is available to argue against each of these statements. And yet many churches are formed on one or more of these positions.

The book of Numbers presents a classic example of an entire group of people acting on disinformation. Joshua and Caleb were sent with ten other men to spy out the land of Canaan. They all agreed that the land flowed with milk and honey and was obviously the land God had promised to them. However, ten of the spies got sidetracked by the apparent strength of the men of the land.

> Then Caleb quieted the people before Moses, and said, "Let us go up at once and take possession, for we are well able to overcome it." But the men who had gone up with him said, "We are not able to go up against the people, for they are stronger than we." And they gave the children of Israel a bad report of the land which they had spied out, saying, "The land through which we have gone as spies is a land that devours its inhabitants, and all the people whom we saw in it are men of great stature. There we saw the giants (the descendants of Anak came from the giants); and we were like grasshoppers in our own sight, and so we were in their sight." (Num. 13:30–33)

The people of Israel did not check the reports from the spies against the promises of the Lord. God was so angry with them, He wanted to destroy the entire nation. Moses convinced Him not to kill them, but God made this pronouncement:

Because all these men who have seen My glory and the signs which I did in Egypt and in the wilderness, and have put Me to the test now these ten times, and have not heeded My voice, they certainly shall not see the land of which I swore to their fathers, nor shall any of those who rejected Me see it. But My servant Caleb, because he has a different spirit in him and has followed Me fully, I will bring into the land where he went, and his descendants shall inherit it. (Num. 14:22-24)

God has given us His Word and His promises, and He expects us to check our decisions and our beliefs with Scripture so that we will not get tripped up with disinformation. The only way to deal with new concepts is to turn to the Word of God, search it out, and ask God to illumine your understanding in these areas. Before you turn God and the power of prayer off, ask God to shed His divine light on your mind, and through His Word help you understand what He wants to teach you in these areas.

Practicing His Presence

1. Have you believed any of the statements listed in this chapter? Which ones?

_____

_____

_____

_____

2. Ask God to show you other areas where you have based your theology on disinformation.

_____

_____

_____

_____

3. Now pray this prayer, and sign and date it to mark your commitment:

Dear Father, I see that some of the wrong opinions I have formed about You and Your Word have kept me from praying effectively. I confess this sin to You. I promise before You right now that I will search out the Scriptures and I will base my opinions about You and Christianity on what Your Word says. Please fill my mind and my heart with Your discerning light. In Jesus' Name. Amen.

_____   _____
NAME   DATE

4. As God reveals the untruth of theological opinions you have
   formed, write down His truth in the space below.

_____

_____

_____

_____

10

Disbelief

While I realize all of these hindrances to praying I have cited in the last several chapters are very real—after talking with many people and tabulating hundreds of surveys—I have come to the conclusion that none of these issues is really strong enough to keep us from praying. There has to be more.

I believe we pray for the wrong reasons. Most people look at prayer as a one-way interaction between them and a generally silent God. We use prayer to log our wants and our complaints. Occasionally we get "lucky"; our wants are supplied or a wrong is made right in our eyes. Then we pursue our pattern of prayer until a request is not answered according to our plan. We may weather one or two more "denials," but soon our interest lags and we quit praying. I think we often regard prayer as a lucky number which we are willing to play until it doesn't work anymore.

I believe the underlying reason most Christians don't pray is that we don't believe God really hears us. If we truly believed that every time we bow our heads and address God by name we instantly have a private audience with the Creator of the entire universe—who has control of everything in and around us and that He not only will listen to us, but desires to converse with us—we would overcome any and all obstacles to talk with Him as often as possible.

First, I can assure you, from Scripture I have included in this book and from my personal experience, that God does want to speak with us and it is truly possible to have a two-way conversation with Him.

Don't let this be true of you: ". . . says the LORD, 'and I spoke to you, rising up early and speaking, but you did not hear, and I called you, but you did not answer'" (Jer. 7:13). Don't miss the opportunity for heavenly interaction because you are not willing to listen for His voice.

Second, I believe we give up on praying because we don't feel our prayers get answered. Recently, I was in the process of returning from a week-long trip. At that same time, as Glen was coming home from church, God spoke to him and said, "Pray for all of the mechanisms on Marilyn's plane."

Unbeknownst to Glen, God had also impressed me to cover every part of my trip in prayer. I was not fearful, simply aware and cautious. I did observe that the airline people seemed to be extra careful on that trip. We waited twice for the plane to be de-iced, and I noticed inspectors checking in the cockpit and all around the plane.

Other than the delays for de-icing, my trip was uneventful. At first I didn't even mention my concerns to Glen, but finally he told me how the Lord had impressed him to pray, and he asked if I had sensed any problems. As we talked, we realized I had obviously been facing some very real danger, and God had not only protected me and answered our prayers, He had even told us we needed to pray!

Rather than thank God for His intervention in our lives, we often take occurrences such as this very passively. We may even say, "Well, nothing happened, so I guess my impression or instinct was wrong." No, it wasn't wrong. God had His angels at the ready to intervene on our behalf, but they needed the power of our prayers to put them into motion.

In the book of Daniel, an angel comes after Daniel had been praying for three weeks.

Then said he unto me, Fear not, Daniel: for from the first day that thou didst set thine heart to understand, and to chasten thyself before thy God, thy words were heard, and I am come for thy words. But the prince of the kingdom of Persia withstood me one and twenty days:

but, lo, Michael, one of the chief princes, came to help me; and I remained there with the kings of Persia. (Daniel 10:12–13 KJV).

Commentator Morris Cerullo states:

In these passages we discover that Daniel's supplications to God were heard by Him from the very first day that Daniel set his heart to purity of purpose and uttered his prayers. But then the invisible war was set in motion. The "prince of the kingdom of Persia," who is the devil or Satan, held back God's emissary who was sent to deliver the answer. For 21 days a great struggle took place in the heavenlies between the forces of God and the forces of Satan before Daniel saw his ultimate victory.[1]

Apparently Daniel's persistence in prayer sustained the angel so that he could fight against the prince of Persia and bring the answer to Daniel. I believe God would desire that we be as persistent as Daniel and never give up. We have no idea whether an invisible war is raging on our behalf.

How many times have you just missed an accident or escaped physical injury? Happenstance? Of course not. God has heard us pray for protection and He is answering our prayers constantly.

Often, if our prayer is not answered the way we expected it to be, we say "My prayer wasn't answered." But God promises, "Call to Me, and I will answer you, and show you great and mighty things, which you do not know" (Jer. 33:3). He always answers, but not always in the way we expect. And at least for myself, I am grateful that He gives me what I need rather than just what I ask for.

Spurgeon commented:

It is neither desirable nor possible that all things should be left to our choice. So much do I feel this, that if my Lord should say to me, "From this hour I will always answer your prayer just as you pray it," the first petition I would offer would be, "Lord, do nothing of the sort." That would be putting the responsibility of my life on myself, instead of allowing it to remain on God.[2]

If God did everything we asked, just as we asked, we wouldn't really need God; a genie in a magic lamp would suffice. The wonderful thing about serving an all-powerful, all-knowing God is that we can trust Him to give us the very best in spite of what we ask for.

We should all join with the father of the possessed son in the book of Mark in saying "Lord, I believe; help my unbelief!" (Mark 9:24).

Practicing His Presence

1. Pray this prayer today:
   Father God, I confess my unbelief. I confess my anger when
   you did not answer my prayers "according to my will."
   Forgive me for trying to control You.

   Father, I surrender to Your will. I commit myself to be faithful
   in praying and in asking. Give me the strength to accept Your
   answers. Help thou my unbelief. In Jesus' Name, Amen.

2. Write your prayer today reminding Him of the prayers you
   think have not been answered.

   _____

   _____

   _____

   _____

3. Tell God how you feel and ask Him to show you whether you
   have missed His answer or if the answer is still forthcoming.

Part

3

THE PRINCIPLES OF TWO-WAY PRAYER

11

A Conversation with God

I have discussed much already about hearing God's voice and listening to Him. I have also referred often to the importance of writing our prayers. For this section on the Principles of Prayer, I want to begin by showing you how this section developed.

After I saw the results of the prayer questionnaire I had distributed, I realized I had to have a section in this book on how we know we are hearing God's voice. That sounded really easy until I sat down to write it. In my prayer journal on November 17, 1992, I wrote: "Lord, please help me know how to start with my book. Help me to touch the needs of the people. Father, please give me direction on how I know it's Your voice I hear."

Then I sat quietly, and the following comparison/contrast outline began to take shape.

CHRIST	SATAN
Convicts	Condemns
Clarifies	Confuses
Confirms	Contradicts
Chooses	Captures
Constrains	Constricts

Then I also heard that still, small voice whisper to me, "My sheep know my voice."

I was quite amazed at such a concise outline. I thanked the Lord for it, but because of time constraints was not able to go further with it that day.

The next day as I was writing in my journal, the Lord spoke to me again, "I will give you the verses for your comparison/contrast outline. Be bold. Don't be afraid to present what I give you."

Those words spurred me on, and I began to check my outline with Scripture. As I searched through Scripture, I was thrilled to see that Scripture confirmed my outline, often even using the actual words the Lord gave me. In the rest of this section, you will see how I was able to develop this entire section from the words the Lord gave me as I was writing in my prayer journal on November 17. The Lord most definitely speaks to us today, but Satan tries to talk to us, too. Satan can sidetrack us through various avenues. He uses our own natural, fleshy desires to tempt us. "Watch and pray, lest you enter into temptation. The spirit indeed is willing, but the flesh is weak" (Matt. 26:41).

We can also be tempted by the voices of this world. "Do not love the world or the things in the world.... For all that is in the world—the lust of the flesh, the lust of the eyes, and the pride of life—is not of the Father but is of the world" (1 John 2:15-16). While we may hear many voices trying to lure us away from God's perfect plan, it is important to realize that the real voice behind them all is Satan. The following chapters will discuss how we can recognize the genuine in a world of counterfeits.

12

Christ Convicts/ Satan Condemns

Many times as I pray with people I will hear them taking all of the blame upon themselves for someone else's actions. Especially if they have been abused as children, they will often see themselves as "bad" people whom Christ could not possibly love or forgive. Some even admit they hear a voice inside saying, "You are bad. How could you have done such a bad thing? Your sin is beyond forgiving. You are bad, bad, bad."

As they tell me what they are hearing, I share this test with them. Christ convicts; Satan condemns.

Christ will say, "What you *did* is bad. The sin is bad, but I love you."

When Christ stood with the woman who had been accused of adultery, He suggested those without sin should cast the first stone. His words did not condemn the people; His words simply convicted their hearts:

> Then those who heard it, being convicted by their conscience, went
> out one by one, beginning with the oldest even to the last. And Jesus
> was left alone, and the woman standing in the midst. When Jesus had

raised Himself up and saw no one but the woman, He said to her, "Woman, where are those accusers of yours? Has no one condemned you?" She said, "No one, Lord." And Jesus said to her, "Neither do I condemn you; go and sin no more." (John 8:9-11)

Satan, however, is in the business of condemning us every chance he gets. In his first letter to Timothy, Paul warns that a bishop or leader should not be a novice in leadership, "lest being puffed up with pride he fall into the same condemnation as the devil" (1 Tim. 3:6).

We need to recognize the temptations and condemnations of Satan and be able to separate them from the warnings and convictions Christ will bring into our lives.

In Scripture Satan is often presented as the accuser of the brethren:

Then I heard a loud voice saying in heaven, "Now salvation, and strength, and the kingdom of our God, and the power of His Christ have come, for the accuser of our brethren, who accused them before our God day and night, has been cast down." (Rev. 12:10)

As Christians we are the targets of those accusations day and night from Satan, our constant foe. As I prayed with a young woman, Jesus walked her through a scene in which she had been sexually abused by a family member. She told me she was very aware of Jesus' presence and she could see Him holding her as a hurting, confused little child. I suggested she listen to what Jesus was saying to that little girl. She was quiet for a few minutes, and then a big smile spread across her face.

"Do you know what He said to me?" she asked.

I shook my head no.

"He told me it wasn't my fault. I am not a bad girl!"

Most of her life, this young woman had heard a voice telling her she was bad and it was all her fault; however, when she asked God for discernment in this matter, she was able to receive Christ's words of comfort and release.

When the voice you hear is condemning you—attacking you as a person, declaring you useless and unfit—according to Scripture, you can renounce that voice because that is the voice of Satan. You do not need to receive his words.

Christ's voice will expose your sin, but He will not expound on how bad you are. Christ's voice will urge us to rid ourselves of sin and He will draw us toward confession and cleansing, but He will never give us the feeling that we as His children are bad. As human beings we have the ability to choose to do bad things, but Christ looks upon His children with love and compassion, never with condemnation.

In an earlier chapter, I referred to the bellhop Joe who felt bad things were happening to him because God was mad at him. Bad things were happening to Joe because he made wrong choices, but right in the middle of all of his mess, God was calling to him, convicting him of his sin, and wooing him to Himself. God loathes our sin, but He loves us. Christ convicts; Satan condemns.

Practicing His Presence

1. When you are trying to talk to God, do you hear words of conviction or words of condemnation? Write down the words of conviction.

_____

_____

_____

_____

Ask God to give you the strength to confess those things and help you to walk His path.

2. Write down the words of condemnation.

_____

_____

_____

_____

Write across this list *Romans 8:1–2*. Pronounce yourself free from these condemning words. Jesus has set you free!

13

Christ Clarifies/ Satan Confuses

Satan uses the standards of this world to confuse us. Recently Glen and I counseled with several couples where the husband is convinced he should leave his wife. Each one's reasoning? "I don't love her anymore because she doesn't meet my needs." These men have been Christians for many years, yet Satan has confused their minds so much that they actually think they are hearing God's voice telling them to leave their wives. They have listened to the "me" philosophy for so long they are beginning to think it is doctrinally sound!

I counseled with a young couple who had been drawn together for all of the wrong reasons. She knew he had a problem with infidelity, with alcoholism, and with pornography. However, he felt a strong call to the ministry and she felt she could help him clean up his act and become a successful minister. She had many vices he was going to help her get rid of also. Against the counsel of their church and the advice of their friends, they got married. Of course they have had nothing but problems, so they came to me stating, "We think perhaps God doesn't want us to be together, and we think it is His will for us to get a divorce."

Satan had them so confused that they had everything backward. It wasn't correct to blame the probable divorce on God; what they should have recognized was it wasn't God's will for them to get married in the first place when they brought so much sin they hadn't dealt with into the union. However, now that they are married, God's rules still hold, and God's Word leaves a very narrow margin for divorce. What they needed to do was confess their sin of disobedience and ask God to shed the light of His Word on their situation and give them divine direction on how to make their marriage work.

Satan will do everything he can to confuse us with worldly logic, but we must realize, "This wisdom does not descend from above, but is earthly, sensual, demonic" (James 3:15).

The apostle Paul stated,

> When I was a child, I spoke as a child, I understood as a child, I thought as a child; but when I became a man, I put away childish things. For now we see in a mirror, dimly, but then face to face. Now I know in part, but then I shall know just as I also am known. (1 Cor. 13:11–12)

As young Christians, most biblical concepts are foreign to us. However, as we study God's Word and learn from our spiritual mentors, we begin to understand biblical concepts, and our thoughts are clarified under the light of God's Word.

Hindsight is always twenty-twenty, so it is easier to look back and see how we got confused than it is to sidestep confusion in the present. As I look back over Glen's and my childrearing years, I feel most of the time we allowed Christ to clarify situations and we made good decisions for our children.

However, when our son Matthew received a large scholarship from a major secular university, I now think we allowed Satan to confuse us with a good thing. Matthew is a brilliant young man, and we were thrilled with his accomplishments. We had always assumed our children would attend Christian colleges, but the offer from this prestigious school was so attractive that it seemed foolish to refuse it. Some people even advised us that no Christian school could offer the intellectual challenge a brilliant young man like Matthew needed.

The offer was wonderful, the academic opportunities were unlimited, and Matt loved it, but he bought into a lifestyle that was not pleasing to the Lord while he was there. Thank goodness God opened our eyes quickly and we were able to rectify the situation by asking Matt to leave the university and come home. I know God used that time in his life to grow him into the strong Christian man he is today, but I still think if we hadn't allowed Satan to confuse us with a seemingly good thing we could have avoided some very painful years for our family.

Obviously we will not understand everything about Scripture in our lifetime. But as we seek God's face, study His Word, and seek godly counsel, we come upon what I call the "spiritual aha's" of life. Some of the theological cloud lifts, and we get another glimpse of God's truth. He clarifies our thinking and our thoughts are confirmed in Scripture. We won't have to twist verses or climb out on theological limbs. God will let us touch a corner of His mind, and we will be able to think clearly and function in a way that pleases Him. Christ clarifies; Satan confuses.

Practicing His Presence

1. What dilemma are you facing right now?

_____

_____

_____

_____

2. Ask God to lead you to biblical standards and wise people to direct you. Pray today that God will expose all of Satan's confusion. Pray that He will give you clarity of thought.

_____

_____

_____

_____

14

Christ Confirms/ Satan Contradicts

When we become Christians, our decision will be confirmed in many ways. People will see changes in us. We will notice our desires begin to change. We will have an awareness and insight to spiritual things that we never had before. When God speaks to us, the authenticity of His voice will also be confirmed in various ways.

Many of the people who filled out my prayer questionnaire stated that they felt confident they were hearing God's voice because people and circumstances confirmed what they felt God was saying to them. This is a valid test as long as we are looking to godly people for the confirmation. I have seen that Satan can arrange circumstances so that it looks like we are experiencing "divine intervention"; therefore, we must also make sure the voice we hear is not telling us to do something that would contradict Scripture.

Consider Paul's statement:

I thank my God always concerning you for the grace of God which was given to you by Christ Jesus, that you were enriched in everything by Him in all utterance and all knowledge, even as the testimony of Christ was confirmed in you, so that you come short in no gift, eagerly waiting for the revelation of our Lord Jesus Christ, who will also confirm you to the end, that you may be blameless in the day of our Lord Jesus Christ. (1 Cor. 1:4-8)

Glen and I first visited Campus Crusade for Christ headquarters in 1966 when we attended a Lay Institute for Evangelism there. I was drawn to the people and the ministry immediately. I began to envision what it would be like to be on staff. I felt very strongly that God was leading Glen and me to join the headquarters staff. However, when I told Glen about it, he didn't share my enthusiasm. I tried to sell him on the idea but quickly realized he was not budging.

As I was taking a shower that evening, I talked to the Lord. "Lord, I think I am hearing Your voice, but I know it would be wrong for me to make further moves on this idea unless Glen agrees with me. I am giving this idea and Glen to You. If You want us to consider coming on staff, I am asking that You will confirm my desires by having someone else talk with Glen and that Glen will change his mind without my saying any more."

While I was still in the shower, a close friend knocked on our hotel room door. The friend told Glen he had had a strong urge to come to the hotel that night to talk with us. By the time I finished in the shower, the man was already suggesting to Glen that we join the staff of Campus Crusade. God also used Scripture to speak to Glen: "You did not choose Me, but I chose you and appointed you that you should go and bear fruit, and that your fruit should remain . . ." (John 15:16). Before the week was over, we had applied for staff!

I believe Satan would have loved for me to go ahead of God's plan. By urging Glen to make a decision before he was ready I could have easily turned him off completely and we could have missed God's call on our lives. Satan could have used my enthusiasm (generally a positive attribute) to cause me to contradict God's plan for our lives.

When we are following God's leading, there will be responses that will confirm we are going in the right direction. The disciples experienced that: "And they went out and preached everywhere, the Lord working with them and confirming the word through the accompanying signs" (Mark 16:20).

I talked with a man recently who married his present wife on the rebound of a broken love relationship. He has been in this difficult marriage for several years and has a family. Recently his former girlfriend, the one he has fantasized about for all these years, moved to his town and started working in the same building where he works.

The former girlfriend started calling him occasionally—just to talk and encourage him in his difficult marriage. He needed so much comforting that they started meeting at a coffee shop in another town.

Before this man met me at the church where I was speaking, he had convinced himself that God brought the former girlfriend back into his life to "rescue" him from his difficult marriage. I pointed out that his plan contradicted God's Word. God would not tempt him to leave his wife for another woman since He teaches that kind of behavior is sin. The man didn't like my words, but I suggested he sit with pen in hand, ask God what he should do, tell Satan to be quiet, and listen to God. A few days later, he said "I talked to God and asked Him what I should do. He said, 'Stop the phone calls; don't see the other woman any more, and work on your marriage.'"

Once the man turned from Satan's plan, he was able to see the contradictions in his situation. God says we aren't to covet another man's wife and vice versa, but Satan had convinced him he was dealing with extenuating circumstances which should override God's rules. Satan had managed to blind him to the obvious contradiction. Finally he was willing to recognize the Scriptures that would lead him away from this improper relationship and confirm God's plan for his life.

Often Satan convinces us we can go against God's laws for a "spiritual" reason. Paul warned of this: "The coming of the lawless one is according to the working of Satan, with all power, signs, and lying wonders" (2 Thess. 2:9).

I talked with a young woman who had been preparing for full-time Christian work. She met a man and began to evangelize him. Even though he had not become a Christian—and Scripture clearly teaches we should not be unequally yoked with someone who is not a Christian (2 Cor. 6:14)—she was able to rationalize a defense for marrying him. She felt if she could just show him how much God loved him by the example of her own unconditional love for him, he would undoubtedly become a Christian and everything would be fine.

Unfortunately within a short time after their marriage, he left her for another woman. Soon she was divorced and her hopes for full-time ministry were dashed. If she had only recognized how her own behavior contradicted Scripture, perhaps she could have escaped making such a serious mistake. God's voice would never have instructed her to go against God's own Word.

Often Satan causes us to go along with societal thinking even though it contradicts God's Word. I have a very dear friend who is a practicing lesbian. One day she commented to me, "I appreciate that you accept me as I am. I'm glad you realize I can't help the way I am since I was born like this."

I stopped her immediately and said. "I love you and I accept you as a person, but I don't agree with your lifestyle. I do not believe you were born this way. If you were, then God really played a dirty trick on you."

She looked surprised and said, "What do you mean?"

"I mean, God states very clearly in the Bible that homosexuality and lesbianism are sin. Since they are sin, I don't believe God would create you to naturally desire something and then forbid you to ever function in that manner. He wouldn't contradict Himself. I believe your lesbian tendencies were produced because of damage imposed upon you by other human beings, but you still have a choice as to whether you are going to act on those desires. I don't think you can blame God for your situation."

I was afraid my honesty would alienate me from my friend, but actually the opposite happened. Although she is still in the lesbian lifestyle, she now feels free to share her doubts and struggles with me. She knows she can trust me because I dared to be honest with her.

As Christians we have tried to make love and acceptance synonymous; they are not. We are not unloving to call homosexuality sin; the Bible calls it sin. However, we are unloving if we hate the sinner as well as the sin. Satan's voice comes at us from the radio, the TV screen, the newspaper, and sometimes even from the pulpit, making us feel guilty by cunningly contradicting what God's Word really says. I believe God's voice will tell us to love the homosexual, the adulterer, the murderer, and others, but God's voice will never tell us to approve of their behavior because then God would be in contradiction of His own Word.

Christ's voice will confirm Scripture; Satan's voice contradicts Scripture.

Practicing His Presence

1. As you write your prayer today, ask God to show you whether you have accepted behaviors or philosophies that contradict God's Word. Write down what He brings to your mind.

_____

_____

_____

_____

15

Christ Chooses/
Satan Captures

When we hear Christ's voice, we will be led into freedom. Christ's voice will not have strings attached. We will not have to couch our words or twist our actions to follow God's voice. We are chosen by Him, and there are no strings attached.

We need to be careful not to get "captured" by a good thing. In my book *When Your Dreams Die*, I discuss that those who hurt need to guard against being caught in obsessive behavior. Often after we have gone through a traumatic event, God gives us a ministry to others who are hurting in a similar way. However, if we have not adequately resolved our own issues, God's providing a way for us to use our difficult experiences becomes an obsession with us and it becomes *our* ministry. We become very rigid in our procedures and very possessive of the truths God has given to us.

While we were definitely *chosen* by God to serve in a specific capacity, we soon become *captured* by Satan because our ministry becomes our life and our identity. When we become obsessed by procedures, often the work of the Holy Spirit is limited. While we may still see fruit from our labor, it is safe to say there would have been more and perhaps healthier fruit if we had continued to be an earthen vessel chosen by God, rather than an obsessed vessel captured by Satan's wiles.

Several years ago Florence Littauer and I sat down one afternoon and listed traits we have observed in those who have become obsessive and/or possessive regarding the ministry God has given them.

- They often display inappropriate anger.
- They become secretive about who is in their group.
- They become secretive about what they are learning.
- They become manipulative.
- They become possessive of their ideas.
- They become unbending in their procedures.
- They seem to be threatened by others' success.
- They become very confrontive.
- But they cannot accept personal confrontation.

The gospel of Christ is straightforward and uncomplicated and so is the Christian life. As you read through Scripture, I think you will observe what I have observed: God gives us lots of do's, but very few don'ts. There truly is freedom in Christ. When we become too involved in the don'ts of Christianity, Satan captures minds and sidetracks us on peripheral issues.

When I was a child I attended a church that nearly split because one of the Sunday school teachers wore lipstick. Today we see the church collective being torn apart over such issues as whether Christians should speak in tongues, utilize emotional healing prayer, "picture" Jesus, picket against abortion, use taped music in their church services, and other similar issues. While these issues all have merit and can probably be effectively argued on both sides, I believe Satan has sidetracked us. He has allowed us to be "captured" in controversy within the body to sap much of our energy—so that we are too tired to share the gospel with a needy world or to spend time letting God speak to us.

Paul wrote, "He chose us in Him before the foundation of the world, that we should be holy and without blame before Him in love" (Eph. 1:4). I understand this verse to mean that Christ chose each one of us individually and He will hold us accountable to be holy and blameless individually. I am glad God created us uniquely and wants to use us uniquely. Certainly, there are specific guidelines in Scripture regarding Christian behavior, but, within those guidelines, God allowed for a lot of individual creativity.

When we get sidetracked on minor issues, we walk right into Satan's trap. The apostle Paul warned, "Do not give the devil a foothold" (Eph. 4:27 NIV).

We should pray for ourselves and others "that they [we] may come to their [our] senses and escape the snare of the devil, having been taken captive by him to do his will" (2 Tim. 2:26).

Christ chooses; Satan captures.

Practicing His Presence

1. As you write your prayer today, ask God to reveal areas where you have been sidetracked and captured by Satan. Write down the thoughts He gives you.

_____

_____

_____

_____

2. In your prayer time, confess these things to Jesus, renounce Satan's devices, and demand that you be released to serve Jesus freely and uniquely as one of His chosen ones—in the name of Jesus.

_____

_____

_____

_____

16

Christ Constrains/ Satan Constricts

I have been working at a breakneck pace for the past few months. My speaking schedule accelerated, the deadline on this book was coming up, and the two back-to-back retreats that Marita Littauer and I run both had record-breaking registrations for this year—and I do all of the registrations for both retreats. The book deadline, the retreats, and five consecutive weekends of speaking converged on me all at once. I became physically exhausted.

In this worn-out condition, I have been very vulnerable to Satan's vicious attacks. In an attempt to revitalize myself spiritually, I began reading Peter Wagner's book *Prayer Shield*.

I was very interested in his discussion on prayer intercessors and how strategic it is for pastors and other Christian workers to have two or three special prayer intercessors. I was lying on my bed in a cabin at a retreat where I was the main speaker when I read a passage in which Wagner described his own prayer intercessors. I was so tired that I quickly fell asleep, but I remember saying to God just before I drifted off, "I sure wish I had someone to intercede for me."

That evening the message went very well, and many women came forward with spiritual needs. I prayed with them for over two hours, until well after 11:00 P.M. As I was about to leave the chapel, however, a young woman came up to me and said, "I'm not sure how to say this, but I believe God has told me tonight that I should be your prayer intercessor."

She then told me she also was reading Wagner's book *Prayer Shield*. I left that retreat curious about this young woman, about intercessory prayer, and about how God was going to use it in my life. I hoped my discouragement would leave and everything would run smoothly now that I had someone to pray specifically for me.

On the contrary, I fell into a very deep depression for the next several days and spent most of my time crying. I was nearly convinced that I should quit speaking, stop writing this book, and just retire into grandmotherhood. I felt God had left me. I sat in a chair in my office and wept, "God, I'm too tired. I'm ready to give up. If You are hearing me, please let me know that You care."

Well, of course, Satan came down on me like a vulture. "How could God ever use someone with such a negative attitude? He must really be ashamed of you!"

I felt so alone and ignored. Then after Satan's little number, I felt ashamed and caught in his trap. After all, how *could* God ever use me?

Well, I was defeated, but the events of the day showed me that God was not defeated; He was aware of me; and He still loved me.

I turned to the devotion in *My Utmost for His Highest* for that morning, and as I read the Bible verse, I burst out laughing. It was John 6:67: "Then Jesus said to the twelve, 'Do you also want to go away?'" Oh, what a stinger! And I realized Jesus was asking me, "Are you going to leave me, too?"

First, I laughed, then I cried, and finally I confessed my sin of depression and discouragement to the Lord. I told Him I was going to walk by faith because I was still tired and worn out, but I had been abruptly reminded that Jesus wants me to stay with Him. He cares about me. I still asked Jesus to have His angels minister to me during that day because I really needed help.

While I was doing prayer counseling with someone that morning, my prayer intercessor left a message on my answering machine that she had been interceding for me all morning. Later that day another woman who prays for me consistently called to say that God really laid me on her heart, and she had been praying for me all morning.

The next morning I found a beautiful terra cotta planter on my porch. A little clay angel was sitting on the corner of the square planter, and the planter contained a miniature rose bush with three tiny pink roses in bloom. Since I do not know who sent it, I have just received it as a special delivery gift from God.

"For the love of Christ constrains us" (2 Cor. 5:14). Oh, how the love of God constrains me! While Satan tries to constrict me and limit my effectiveness through any means, God quietly encourages people to pray for me and deposits angels and rosebuds at my door. Christ constrains; Satan constricts.

Practicing His Presence

1. Do you need evidence of God's constraining love today? Is Satan constricting the flow of God's power in you? How?

_____

_____

_____

_____

2. In your prayer today, tell Jesus how you feel. Ask Him to reveal His love for you in even a small way today. Then pray that He will open your eyes and heart to be able to receive His gifts of love.

_____

_____

_____

_____

Part

4

THE PURPOSE OF PRAYER

17

Inspiration

Why do we pray? I think if most of us were honest we would say we pray because we need something. Generally when we think of prayer, we think of our talking to God because our prayers are often monologues rather than dialogues. We talk to God, but we seldom sit still long enough for Him to respond. Prayer should be a two-way interaction. First, we must consider our part in the purpose of prayer.

Our part of prayer should contain praise. Psalm 34:3 says, "Oh, magnify the LORD with me, and let us exalt His name together." Praise the Holy One you serve, the Sovereign Lord, the King. Praise Him for Who He is. We should enter "into His courts with praise" (Ps. 100:4).

Perhaps each day you might want to focus on a specific attribute of God and praise Him for that attribute and how it has affected your life.

Gracious heavenly Father, I praise You for Your faithfulness to me. You are ever present. You never leave me alone. You are never too busy for me. You are a faithful God who is always conscious of me.

Father, I thank You that even though humans have let me down, You never let me down. Even when I am not faithful to You, You are always faithful to me. Praise You, Jesus.

Next the psalmist said, "Let us come before His presence with thanksgiving" (Ps. 95:2). I don't think our prayers need to be rote lists of "Thank You for Mommy, Daddy, brother, sister, my pet bunny" as a little child might say, but I do think we should thank the Lord for His provisions and His protection of us and our families.

Later in this book I tell the story of how long we waited for our little grandson Christian Josiah to arrive in our family. He is definitely a special gift from God. Since Christian's birth, I have never heard my son-in-law, Mike, pray without including the statement, "Thank You for our boy." I believe that statement must warm God's heart each time He hears it because it is a reminder to God and to all who hear the prayer that Mike is grateful for God's special blessing when He gave us Christian.

> *Father, I thank You for Your constant provision for me and my family. I thank You that You have given us good jobs so that we can provide for our families. Jesus, I thank You for my children, Matt and Mellyn, for my son-in-law, Mike, and my daughter-in-law, Debbie. I thank You for my precious grandchildren, Kate, Nate, and Christian. I also thank You for my dear husband, Glen. Most of all, Father, I thank You for Your provision of salvation through Your precious son, Jesus Christ. Thank You for allowing me to partake of this eternal gift. You are a wonderful God.*

Third, our prayers should also include worship: "Rejoice in the Lord always. Again I will say, rejoice!" (Phil. 4:4).

Acknowledge Him for Who He is and that we can come into the presence of the Holy God. Worship Him with your eyes toward Him. Just as my little dog looks at me, and his eyes don't leave me, we can be that way with our heavenly Father. Often when I am worshiping the Lord, I sing a hymn or a chorus that expresses how I feel. Such choruses as "We Worship and Adore You" or "I Love You, Lord" are among my favorites.

> *O Lord, You are a great God. I worship You. I adore You. I bow before You. You are the God above all gods. You are worthy of all of my praise and adoration. I am Your servant.*

Once we have looked upward, there should be a time of looking inward. First Peter 4:7 says, "But the end of all things is at hand; therefore be serious and watchful in your prayers." Today we certainly feel that the end of all things could be near, don't we? Every day I am more aware of the possibility that Christ may be coming soon.

Peter tells us we should be serious, or clear-minded. Our introspection time can tell us if our minds and hearts are clear and if we're ready to meet our God in prayer. Are we prepared to live for the Lord? Psalm 139:23-24 states, "Search me, O God, and know my heart;/Try me, and know my anxieties;/And see if there is any wicked way in me,/And lead me in the way everlasting."

We should pray, *Lord, come with me and look in my life. Let's take a housekeeping tour; let's look and see if everything is clean.* And when we find the sin, we can know, "If we confess our sins, He is faithful and just to forgive us our sins and to cleanse us from all unrighteousness" (1 John 1:9). Then we can go on in a good and healthy interaction with Him.

Chambers observes,

> It is never safe to do much introspection, but it is ruinous to do none. Introspection can never satisfy us, yet introspection is not wrong, it is right, because it is the only way we discover that we need God. It is the introspective power in us that is made alert by conviction of sin.[1]

And so as we look in, the Lord says, "There's the sin we have to deal with." We move that out of the way, and we look a little more, and He says, "There's some more" and we become aware of the sin in our lives through the introspection. And as Chambers says, too much can be dangerous. But none will ruin us, because we must be willing to look inside.

Dear Jesus, come with me as we walk through the rooms of my heart. O Holy Spirit, show me any unconfessed sin in my life. Show me where my motives and actions are wrong. Look deep, dear Holy Spirit. Reveal my innermost thoughts. Guide me and be patient with me as I work through the pains of my past, with the wrong habits, with the dysfunctional thought patterns.

I confess each sin to You. I place each sin at the cross and leave it there to be remembered by You no more. Thank You, Jesus.

Once we have spent time in worship, praise, thanksgiving, and confession we are prepared for God's part of prayer. The purpose of prayer is not only that we talk to God, but that we give Him an opportunity to talk with us. As Jesus was preparing for His crucifixion, He said to His disciples, "Sit here, while I pray" (Mark 14:32).

Sue Monk Kidd comments, "*Sit here while I pray.* I looked at the candles glowing in a quiet cluster on the altar and considered those words. Suddenly they became Christ's invitation not only to the disciples but to me. He wanted *me* to sit while he prayed."[2]

I believe part of prayer includes sitting quietly while the Spirit communes with us and in us. This can be difficult because in this world we are almost afraid of silence. We find a protection—a safety—in noise, but the Lord has asked, "Be still, and know that I am God" (Ps. 46:10).

Recently *Time* magazine presented an article entitled "The Eloquent Sounds of Silence."

> We all know how treacherous are words, and how often we use them to paper over embarrassment, or emptiness, or fear of the larger spaces that silence brings. "Words, words, words" commit us to positions we do not really hold, the imperatives of chatter; words are what we use for lies, false promises and gossip. We babble with strangers; with intimates we can be silent. We "make conversation" when we are at a loss; we unmake it when we are alone, or with those so close to us that we can afford to be alone with them.
>
> In love, we are speechless; in awe, we say, words fail us.[3]

Sit silently. Let words fail you as you stand in awe before the Father. Wait for Him to speak. Don't be impatient. Wait for Him.

Our prayer can be this, "Do not keep silent, O God!/Do not hold Your peace,/And do not be still, O God!" (Ps. 83:1).

Spurgeon draws a very beautiful picture of what happens when we pray:

In prayer the heart of man empties himself before God, and then Christ empties his heart out to supply the needs of his poor believing child. In prayer we confess to Christ our deficiencies and he reveals to us his fullness. We tell him our sorrows, he tells us his joys. We tell him our sins, he shows to us his righteousness. We tell him the dangers that lie before us, he tells us of the shield of omnipotence with which he can and will guard us. Prayer talks with God; it walks with him. And he who is much in prayer will hold very much fellowship with Jesus Christ.[4]

Practicing His Presence

1. As you write your prayer today, praise Him for who He is.

_____

_____

_____

_____

2. Thank Him for what He has done for you.

_____

_____

_____

_____

3. Worship Him.

_____

_____

_____

_____

4. Now pray. "Father, look deep inside me today. Shine the light of Your Holy Spirit on my heart. Let me look with You, Father. Expose my sin."

As the Father exposes your sin, confess it to Him, which means to agree with Him. Place yourself at the cross and give your sin to Him.

_____

_____

_____

_____

5. Just sit quietly and bask in His presence. Listen.

_____

_____

_____

_____

18

Instruction

Through prayer we receive instruction. We see the Lord giving us an example of this all the way through His life. He often went away to pray alone and to spend quiet time talking with His Father. He made no decisions without consulting with His heavenly Father, as He states in John, "But I pass no judgment without consulting the Father. I judge as I am told" (John 5:30 TLB).

It appears that He often talked things over more than once. After He already received instructions about His death, Scripture says, "Again, a second time, He went away and prayed, saying, 'O My Father, if this cup cannot pass away from Me unless I drink it, Your will be done'" (Matt. 26:42). And then it says, "So He left them, went away again, and prayed the third time, saying the same words" (Matt. 26:44).

Chambers says that in praying you "tell God what you know He knows, in order that you may get to know it as He does."[1] Now think about that.

We can share our thoughts with Him and say, "Now, is this right? Is this what I understand? This is what I think I know about this. Is it right? I know You're aware of this. Now, feed it back to me." And as we become aware of what God knows, we can pass it back around and it finally becomes part of us. God is so good to us in allowing us time to talk back, to question if we need to, and say, "But have You considered this? And have You thought about that?" Finally, He gets us around to what He knew all the time. What a wonderful, patient, understanding God we serve.

Isaiah 28:26 says, "For He instructs him in right judgment,/His God teaches him." Our goal in receiving instruction should be this: "The LORD GOD has given Me/The tongue of the learned,/That I should know how to speak/A word in season to him who is weary./He awakens Me morning by morning,/He awakens My ear/To hear as the learned" (Isa. 50:4).

As one who hears people's difficult and troubled stories so much of the time, I feel this verse is for me. There are many times I don't know what to say, but I do know the Lord has given me "the tongue of the learned," so I might know the word that sustains the weary. How do you encourage the family who have just buried their child? How do you encourage a woman who has suffered sexual abuse? There are ways, because the Lord has promised to give me and you the words when we are yielded to His leading, and He will awaken our "ear to hear as the learned."

Recently I was praying with a group of women at a retreat when one of the women prayed something like this, "Lord, I hear these women talking about the friendships you have given them, but Lord, I have never felt that kind of love. I have never felt like I belong anywhere. And God, I don't feel like I belong in this group either. I feel so alone."

As I listened to her honest but heart-wrenching prayer, I heard the Lord tell me to go over, lay my hands on this woman, and pray for her. I didn't even know her name, and I wasn't sure how my actions would be received by her or by the rest of the group, but I obeyed God's voice.

As I put my hand on her shoulder, I prayed, "Father, I ask that you would give this dear woman a sense of belonging with You and within this group. I pray she would be released from the bonds that were imposed on her by others in her childhood, the bonds that kept her separate from others." As I prayed those words, I could feel her body relax and she began to cry gently.

When the prayer time was finished, she asked me, "Has anyone told you about me and about my childhood?"

"I don't even know your name, let alone anything about your past," I answered.

The woman explained, "When I was a child I was severely abused. I was isolated from everyone, and I was actually tied down. When you prayed for me to be released from the bonds, I felt the restraints break and I knew I was free."

The Lord gave me the words this young woman needed to hear. He gave me the "tongue to know how to speak a word in season to him who is weary."

I love Psalm 16:7: "I will bless the LORD who has given me counsel;/My heart also instructs me in the night seasons." In CLASS (Christian Leaders, Authors, and Speakers Seminars) we use this verse to teach the conferees how to outline and prepare a message. We give them an assignment for the next day and tell them if they have trouble completing it, they should pray before they go to bed and ask the Lord to instruct their minds in the night. So many of them laugh at us when we say that, but the next morning they are rather chagrined when they come in with an outline that came to their minds while they were asleep. The Lord instructed them in the night!

We can continue fellowship with God even while we're sleeping. Even in the night He can interact with our minds; He can talk with us; and He can change our hearts. Have you ever gone to bed so confused, but you woke up in the morning and could see the solution to your problem? God did a work in your heart and mind in the night. He instructs us even in the night.

Today, I have isolated myself to write and to pray. Dear friends of mine are facing a very serious crisis. I have never practiced fasting, but yesterday the Lord made it very clear to me I am to fast today and uphold my friends in prayer.

Today the Lord gave me very simple, but specific, instructions: "Trust Me, and speak the truth." All day long I have heard those words, "trust" and "truth."

When we place ourselves before the Father, He will give us clear and simple instructions, instructions that we can follow.

Practicing His Presence

1. Do you need specific instructions today? Write a letter expressing your needs to Jesus and then write down the verses He gives you or the words He puts in your mind. Wait on Him and He will instruct you. Always compare what you hear with Scripture.

_____

_____

_____

_____

_____

_____

_____

_____

_____

19

Intercession

Have you had times when you have tried to pray and nothing would come out? I have had times I've just literally said, "Holy Spirit, you take it. I don't know what to say. You just talk to God about this." And I sit there and am quiet and just let the Lord interact with the Holy Spirit. Since I don't know what to say, I can't explain what is going on. I just trust the Holy Spirit and God to interact on the issue and that they are in control. The Holy Spirit can express the words that I cannot express.

Intercession by the Holy Spirit for us is one of the most exciting tools God has given us. Romans 8:26 says, "Likewise the Spirit also helps in our weaknesses. For we do not know what we should pray for as we ought, but the Spirit Himself makes intercession for us with groanings which cannot be uttered."

God has also shown me that we can intercede for people even when we don't know them. When I was a teenager, I watched Billy Graham on television as he was presenting a message for young people. He challenged teenagers to pray for their future partners, even if they had no idea who this was going to be. As a young teen, I decided to accept his challenge. It at least gave me comfort that maybe there was going to be a future partner if I was praying for him. So I started praying for this person I would marry, and I prayed all through my teenage years. Glen attended college in Michigan when he was eighteen. He met my family at that time, but he did not meet me for nearly a year since I was in college in Indiana, where he was from. My father was the teacher of the college-age class at our church, and he called on Glen. My dad eventually had part in leading Glen to Jesus Christ; then my dad introduced Glen to me.

Even though Glen was not a Christian when he came to Michigan, his family had started going to church when he was in his early teens. Therefore, he was open to the invitation from a college classmate to attend church with him, especially when his friend told him the church had "lots of really cute girls!"

As we traced it back, we believe it was the summer I started praying for the man I would marry that Glen's family started going to church. You see, we can intercede when we don't even know whom we are praying for. You can pray for people in your life; you can pray for people who are going to be future generations of your family. We have power in intercession.

Chambers observes, "By intercessory prayer, we can hold off Satan from other lives and give the Holy Spirit a chance with them. No wonder Jesus put such tremendous emphasis on prayer."[1] As children of God who know how to relate to the heavenly Father, we have the power to hold off Satan so that the Holy Spirit can do His work in others and in ourselves. That's a tremendous power. Unfortunately, I don't think we use it very often.

Chambers warns, "The prominent people for God are marked for the wiles of the devil and we must pray for them all the time. God gives us every now and again, an alarming exhibition of what happens if we don't."[2]

That comment makes me feel Chambers lived in our day rather than in the early 1900s, for he certainly gives a description of the Christian community that would fit now. If we've ever had an alarming exhibition of what happens when the Christian community is obviously not praying enough for leaders, we have had it within the last few years as we've seen Christian leaders fall all around us.

Peter Wagner, in his book *Prayer Shield*, focuses on the need for pastors and Christian leaders to be covered by prayer intercessors.

In order to illustrate the wide scope of our ignorance as a Christian community on the power of personal intercession, I want to pick up once again on the current epidemic of pastors and other leaders falling into sexual immorality. The scandals have become so widespread and so public that several Christian authors have been researching and writing on the subject. I have made a personal collection of this material because I began to notice a trend reflecting our ignorance of the power of personal intercession.[3]

In the next several paragraphs Wagner cites many different Christian periodicals and books which address the issue of immorality in the ministry and give suggestions as to how such situations could be avoided. He observes that not one of the authors mentions prayer as a preventative.

Wagner gives the following conclusion:

> To summarize, it does not seem to occur to these leaders, whose stature is so widely respected, to advocate personal intercession as one of the means for preventing pastors from falling into sexual immorality. Why? It apparently simply never occurred to them. This is what I mean when I say that ignorance is the number one reason why we have not been using personal intercession as we should.[4]

We all need intercessory prayer: "Therefore I exhort first of all that supplications, prayers, intercessions, and giving of thanks be made for all men" (1 Tim. 2:1).

Not that you are going to see all of the answers right now, but we are commanded to pray, and to pray for others. Chambers points out: "Intercession does not develop the one who intercedes, it blesses the lives of those for whom he intercedes. The reason so few of us intercede is because we don't understand this."[5]

You see, if I had prayed and wanted to see an answer right away about my future husband, I could have said, "Well, this doesn't work. I haven't met anybody yet who is going to marry me. And I don't know who he is. So maybe I should give up praying." But my prayers were benefiting Glen, even though I didn't know what was going on. Don't get discouraged because you don't see the effects of your prayers. The people may look just the same on the outside and we may think our prayers aren't having any effect, but we can't see how the person is affected on the inside. We can believe our God. He is going to answer our intercessory prayers, even if the answers don't come before we die. We can still trust He will continue to intercede in our situation, and that He is in control and has heard our prayers.

Another way we can intercede in prayer is by creating a legacy for our family, our children, and our grandchildren. I heard a well-known minister say years ago that if he were to die that day, his children would be all prayed up. And when he said that, I thought, *What in the world does he mean, "all prayed up"?* He said that he had prayed his children through grade school, high school, college, marriage, choosing their partners, their vocation, and everything he could think of that they might do in their lives. He had them all prayed up. You see, those prayers would continue to be effective even if the minister died.

I thought to myself, *I like that idea.* So I started praying for my children. I prayed for them even before they were born, but then I started praying about whom they were going to marry. As I had problems with my kids and met crossroads in the childrearing years, I would say, "Oh, Lord, whoever it is they are going to marry, if their parents are going through this right now, please help them have the wisdom to know what to do! And please help these kids come to a saving knowledge of You." Even though I didn't know who they were going to marry, I still prayed for them.

Well, the Lord put my future son-in-law at our door when he was in the ninth grade. The Lord let me answer part of my own prayer as I began to make a spiritual investment in this dear young man. Of course, I didn't know that was what I was doing. Mike started coming to our house for meals and going in the camper with us to the beach. I would share Christ with this boy, and I continued for years. He just couldn't understand how we could be such nice people and believe such crazy things. But he still liked us. The food was good at our house and our daughter was cute, so he kept coming back. He was not dating Mellyn at the time because he knew we wouldn't allow him to since he wasn't a Christian. But Mellyn would sit over in a corner and watch him interact with her mother and wish that he would pay attention to her.

He came to our house when he was a senior in college, and I said, "What are you doing here today? Did you come to see your mom?"

He said, "No, I've come to see you. I don't know what's happened, but I know now for sure that there's a God. Now I need you to tell me the rest."

So I started telling him the rest. It took from August to March to convince this boy of his need for a Savior, but finally he called me one day, and said, "Well, I thought you ought to be the first to know."

I said, "When did you receive the Lord?"

"Four days ago."

"Why didn't you call me right away?"

He said, "Well, I wanted to make sure it worked!"

It worked, and oh, the joy that we have had watching him grow in the Lord. I am writing this chapter on the twelfth anniversary of his spiritual birth. He now teaches two Bible studies each week, one to a group of young couples and the other to a group of inmates.

About three weeks after Mike became a Christian, he called me and asked, "Can I date her now?" How could we refuse? We had loved Mike for so long that he already seemed like part of our family. We were thrilled to have him date our daughter, Mellyn. In just a few months they were engaged, and they were married a year later. While I didn't give physical birth to him, I truly love him as though he were my son. After all, I interceded in prayer for him for nearly nine years. Now that is a long labor!

Now I pray for my three grandchildren in the same way, and I'm already praying for their future partners. Regardless of how long I am on this earth, I want to make sure my children and my grandchildren are "all prayed up."

Chambers states, "There is nothing to be valued more highly than to have people praying for us. God links up His power in answer to their prayers."[6] He also says, "You were born into this world and will probably never know to whose prayers your life is the answer."[7]

What an opportunity we have in prayer. Through prayer, we can invest in the future. People can be born long after we're gone, but we can have an investment in them, in their lives, and in their families through our prayers.

There is a scriptural basis for creating a legacy of prayer. The Lord Jesus Christ said, "I do not pray for these alone [referring to the disciples], but also for those who will believe in Me through their word" (John 17:20). So He prayed far beyond His time on earth. He prayed "also for those who will believe in Me because of their word." Do you realize what a legacy of prayer has come down through the ages? Somehow we are connected to Peter and Paul and John, and all of those people the Lord prayed for while He was on earth—that is a legacy.

Think about the people for whom you should be creating a legacy. In whose life would you like to invest? Children, grandchildren, great-grandchildren? Prayer knows no time. It has no limits. It will be effective once we utter it, even after we are gone.

Practicing His Presence

1. Think of some people in whose lives you want to invest by praying for them and by creating a legacy of prayer for them. Write down the names of those for whom you wish to create a legacy of prayer. Let God direct you in how you should pray for each person.

_____

_____

_____

_____

_____

_____

_____

_____

_____

_____

_____

_____

_____

Part

5

THE
PROCESS OF
PRAYER

20

Separation

It is important that we learn to separate ourselves whenever possible for the purpose of praying. We need to have a cloistered mind. I don't know what you think of when you think of the word *cloistered*, but what I see is someone pulled in, covered, separated from others. In some of the monasteries, the outside halls are called cloisters. Cloistered means being separated. It can mean physically, but also I believe it can mean just having our minds separated from what's going on around us. We can pull our minds in and concentrate on God. Even when we are in a crowd, we can have that cloistered time with the Lord.

Paul just simply said, "Pray without ceasing" (1 Thess. 5:17). Pray continually—in the car, in the shower, at work. I found I can cloister my mind when I am exercising at the gym. I hate exercise; my husband and I, however, have gotten to the point where it is a necessity. For over a year we went to the gym at 5:30 A.M., three days a week. The 5:30 part made it even worse. If it had been 8 or 9 o'clock in the morning it wouldn't have been quite so bad. But 5:30 was just really a terrible time for me to have to be at the gym. I sat there pedaling that bicycle, hating every minute of it, until I began to realize, *You've got twenty-five minutes of pedaling this bicycle that you can pray. Shut out the bicycle, get the feet going in motion, and then just pray.*

I was actually able to close out everything around me. I didn't even notice the noise or the blaring music. I was able to cloister, to separate my mind, and the pedaling time became a time for me and the Lord.

Driving a car can also be that way. Of course, we can't be so separated that we don't pay attention to our driving. But there is a lot of driving that is automatic. Sometimes we find ourselves turning the radio on or doing other things just to keep noise going. Well, why not make the noise yourself instead?

Talk out loud to the Lord. When you're in the car all by yourself and no one else can hear you, use that time for the Lord.

The Lord gave us the example of separating ourselves from others:

And when He had sent the multitudes away, He went up on the mountain by Himself to pray. Now when evening came, He was alone there. (Matt. 14:23)

Now in the morning, having risen a long while before daylight, He went out and departed to a solitary place; and there He prayed. (Mark 1:35)

And when He had sent them away, He departed to the mountain to pray. (Mark 6:46)

So He Himself often withdrew into the wilderness and prayed. (Luke 5:16)

Do you see the pattern that He set for us? He pulled away from the crowd and even from His disciples.

Spurgeon comments,

I cannot help praying. If I were not allowed to utter a word all day long, that would not affect my praying. If I could not have five minutes that I might spend in prayer by myself, I should pray all the same. Minute by minute, moment by moment, somehow or other, my heart must commune with my God. Prayer has become as essential to me as the heaving of my lungs and the beating of my pulse.[1]

It is possible to "pray without ceasing"; we can be in constant prayer. Even now as I am writing, God and I are conversing. I'm asking Him to give me the words that need to come out, and I'm sensing what He is saying to me.

Chambers observes,

> It is impossible to live the life of a disciple without definite times of secret prayer. You will find that the place to enter in is in your business, as you walk along the street, in the ordinary ways of life, when no one dreams you are praying, and the reward comes openly, a revival here, a blessing there.[2]

There have been times when I've been having difficulty talking with someone. Right then I have prayed, and said, "Lord, just intervene. Get this thing going in the right direction." And it has happened right there without anyone realizing what took place. Onlookers have said, "Boy, that person's attitude sure turned around, didn't it? Wasn't that strange how things changed there?" It happened just because of those prayers of "Lord, are You aware of what's going on here? This needs to go in another direction. Let's get this stopped." God will intervene as we walk along the street, as we are in our workplace, wherever we are, as we have that constant relationship with Him.

If you don't have constant communication with Him, as well as those very solitary moments when you can enter into your own personal prayer closet at home or wherever it is, you are in extreme spiritual peril. We cannot survive without constant interaction with God. We are in danger if we think we can pull that off because we can't. We will be so vulnerable to the spirits around us if we don't communicate constantly in our relationship with God. We must nurture a mind that is set apart, separate, cloistered for Him.

C. S. Lewis states:

> An ordinary, simple Christian kneels down to say his prayers. He is trying to get in touch with God. But if he is a Christian he knows that what is prompting him to pray is also God: God, so to speak, inside him. But he also knows that all his real knowledge of God comes through Christ, the Man who was God—that is Christ standing beside him, helping him to pray, praying for him. You see what is happening.

God is the thing to which he is praying—the goal he is trying to reach. God is also the road or bridge along which he is pushed to that goal. . . . [T]he whole threefold life of the three-personal Being is actually going on in that ordinary little bedroom where an ordinary man is saying his prayers.[3]

The next time you pray, think about what is going on. As you pray, you have the undivided attention of the Father, the Son, and the Holy Spirit. Each part of the Trinity is actively involved in some unique way in every prayer you utter. Take time to drink in that concept.

The above quote from Lewis just gives us a glimpse of the process on the heavenly side of prayer. But what about the process from our side? Often we get so hung up on the physical expectations and posture that we forget what prayer is all about. As we enter into prayer we instantly have a private audience with the God and Creator of the entire universe. His total attention is focused on us. We don't have to vie for His attention as we might if we were one of many children in a large family. He treats each of His children as though he or she were His only child.

According to Spurgeon:

You see the men in the belfry sometimes down below with the ropes. They pull them, and if you have no ears, that is all you know about it. But the bells are ringing up there. They are talking and discoursing sweet music up aloft in the tower. And our Prayers do, as it were, ring the bells of heaven. They are sweet music in God's ear.[4]

Have you considered that your prayers are sweet music in God's ear? Prepare your heart to ring the bells of heaven with your prayers today.

Through this book we have learned about who God is. He is the Principal of prayer. Without God, prayer would not work. He is the hub that makes the wheel turn.

We have discussed the various problems of prayer and have been encouraged to confess our sins of unbelief. We have learned to identify the counterfeit by becoming intimate with the genuine. We have acquired principles of prayer that will help us know the difference between Satan's and God's voice.

We have studied the purpose of prayer, mainly that we might glorify the Father, interact with Him, and intercede for others.

Now we are ready to practice the process of prayer. So go to your favorite place to pray. Have your prayer journal or the journal pages of this book with you.

I like Spurgeon's comment: "God the Holy Ghost writes our prayers, God the Son presents our prayers, and God the Father accepts our prayers. And with the whole Trinity to help us in it, what cannot prayer perform?"[5]

Now let me pray this prayer for you from Ephesians 1:18–19: "[I pray also that] the eyes of your understanding being enlightened; that you may know what is the hope of His calling, what are the riches of the glory of His inheritance in the saints, and what is the exceeding greatness of His power toward us who believe...."

Father God, I pray this prayer along with the apostle Paul for myself and for all who are reading this little handbook on prayer. Come, Holy Spirit, and quicken our minds that we might receive Your thoughts; open the eyes of our heart that we might see Jesus; unstop our ears that we might hear our Father's voice. We come as children who have confessed our sin and have been cleansed in the blood of Jesus. We stand in Your presence now, waiting to commune with You. Thank You, Jesus. Amen.

With the eyes of your heart, see that Jesus is there with you. He is waiting to talk with you. Listen for His voice.

Practicing His Presence

1. Ask the Lord to show you times when you could "cloister" your mind and set your thoughts on Him. Write down the thoughts He gives you.

_____

_____

_____

_____

2. Do you have a prayer closet, a place for your private times of prayer? If not, think today of a spot you can make your private praying place.

_____

_____

_____

_____

21

Affection

The greatest words we can hear from our heavenly Father are "I love you," yet they are often the hardest words for us to receive.

Because of emotional damage in our lives, if we are willing to admit it, most of us feel unlovable. It is hard for us to really believe that another human being loves us, let alone that God Himself, the Creator of the entire universe, loves us.

My friend JoAnne writes:

Marilyn had come to our mountain retreat for a few days of R & R and we were discussing prayer and all that it entails.

When I was first introduced to the concept of listening prayer I was a bit apprehensive and a little skeptical.

I had had some traumatic things happen to me as a child and I needed emotional healing from the Lord. As we prayed about them, Marilyn led me and at the end she encouraged me to just stop and listen as the Lord would speak to me; not in an audible voice but through that still, small voice whispering in my heart. And what I heard was "JoAnne, I love you!" I was overcome with tears of joy and for the first time in my life I knew God had healed me from those things done to me as a child.

Since that time I have learned many things from the Lord. [I've experienced] joy in just spending time with Him—patience in waiting for Him to speak to me—enduring times of silence—but most of all a real burden for those who are emotionally hurting as I was.

Remember the main test of discerning whether what we hear is truly God's voice? We must always ask, *Does what I hear agree with Scripture?*

Is it scriptural that God loves you and me? Let's see what Scripture says.

Yes, I have loved you with an everlasting love. (Jer. 31:3)

A new commandment I give to you, that you love one another; as I have loved you, that you also love one another. (John 13:34)

For the love of Christ constrains us. (2 Cor. 5:14)

In this is love, not that we loved God, but that He loved us and sent His Son to be the propitiation for our sins. (1 John 4:10)

There is no fear in love; but perfect love casts out fear, because fear involves torment. But he who fears has not been made perfect in love. We love Him because He first loved us. (1 John 4:18–19)

Does He love you? Oh yes, oh yes!

Now sit quietly with pen in hand and wait to hear those words in your mind and write down what you hear.

At first, you may hear words to the contrary—go ahead and write them down. If you hear words that would cast doubt on God's love for you, read back over the verses I quoted above. Then anything you hear that is contrary to those verses, you can know is a lie from Satan. Write the thought down and then in big letters write across it, THIS IS A LIE. Do that with each negative, unscriptural thought you receive. Ask God to rebuke Satan, and continue to listen for that still, small voice that will back up the Scripture that says, "I have loved you with an everlasting love."

When you hear Jesus say in some form, "I love you," write it down even if you write with a shaky hand. Write it down in faith believing that God and His Word do not lie. Once you have heard God's confirmation of love for you, write across it THANK YOU, JESUS!

Each day listen for Christ's affirmation in your mind that He loves you. His love will never change. Scripture teaches that once we are His children, we can never be separated from His love.

> [Not even] tribulation, or distress, or persecution, or famine, or nakedness, or peril, or sword . . . neither death nor life, nor angels nor principalities nor powers, nor things present nor things to come, nor height nor depth, nor any other created thing, shall be able to separate us from the love of God which is in Christ Jesus our Lord. (Rom. 8:35–39)

Because we are His children, Scripture teaches we can always walk boldly into His presence even if we just need to hear Him say one more time "I love you." Because "In [Him] we have boldness and access with confidence through faith in Him" (Eph. 3:12).

Once again to quote Spurgeon:

> If there is one subject more than another upon which I wish ever to speak, it is the love of Christ. But if there is one which quite baffles me and makes me go back from this platform utterly ashamed of my poor feeble words, it is this subject. This love of Christ is the most amazing thing under heaven, if not in heaven itself.[1]

Receive His love today.

A Conversation with God

"I love you, child."
    You love me?
"You are my precious one."
    How can that be?
"I know your inmost parts."
    And you still love me?
"For my pleasure you were formed."
    Can it really be?
"I love to talk with you."
    You want to talk to me?
"I love to hear your voice."
    Could it possibly be?
He really loves me.
    He just told me so!
Jesus loves me.
    This I know!
Be still—LISTEN.
    He's talking to you and me.
Shh—can you hear Him?
    Stillness is the key.
                    M.W.H. 1993

Practicing His Presence

1. Follow the procedures I suggested in this chapter to hear God's voice and test that it is really His voice. Now thank Jesus for loving you. Write a prayer to Him telling Him of your love for Him. Take time to bask in His love.

_____

_____

_____

_____

_____

_____

_____

_____

22

Reflection

Often when we pray we are in the middle of a problem. As we take our difficulty to the Lord, it will be helpful if we can reflect on the past and recall His faithfulness in the midst of former problems.

In the Old Testament God many times reminded the Israelites of how He had rescued them in the past. "I am the LORD your God who brought you out of the land of Egypt, out of the house of bondage" (Deut. 5:6).

And again, "Remember His marvelous works which He has done,/His wonders and the judgments of His mouth" (1 Chron. 16:12).

God has walked me through many Egypts in my lifetime, but as I was considering this section, the Egypt he brought to my mind was the birth of our granddaughter, Kate.

It was a quiet Saturday morning. I had just finished my Bible reading and was slowly sipping a cup of coffee when the phone rang and abruptly ended my reverie.

"The baby's coming!" announced my son on the other end of the telephone line. I hurried upstairs to tell Glen, "You're going to be a grandpa today!"

Glen and I hurried to get dressed. We gathered up a few personal items in case we had to stay overnight, and we were soon on our way.

During the two-hour drive to our son Matt's town, we silently prayed for our daughter-in-law, Debbie, and for Matt. Occasionally we talked about the changes that were coming. We were going to be grandparents. What fun!

As we walked into the hospital, Glen proudly asked directions to the maternity waiting room and we were directed to the fourth floor. As we stepped off the elevator, we paused for a moment trying to figure which way to turn, and a young man from our son's church walked up to us.

He said, "Mr. and Mrs. Heavilin, I'm here to take you to Matt. The baby has been born, but there were some complications in delivery. Matt is in ICU watching the doctors. They're working with the baby because they're not sure she'll live, and if she does, they fear severe brain damage."

A multitude of thoughts and questions raced through my mind:

Our grandbaby is here—a little girl.

Complications—what kind of complications?

How could anything go wrong? Debbie is so healthy. She took such good care of herself during the pregnancy. She didn't take medication, and she wouldn't even drink coffee or tea!

The baby might not live? Impossible. Absolutely impossible. This couldn't be happening to us again—please, dear Lord, not again. . . .

When we turned the corner, I saw Matt explaining the situation to Debbie's parents who arrived just before us.

Matt came to me and hugged me tightly. We couldn't speak, but our eyes communicated everything we were thinking and feeling. The next few hours seem to be one big blur in my memory. Debbie's parents stayed at the hospital with her, and we went to be with Matt at the children's hospital where our granddaughter, Kate, had been transported.

In the wee hours of the morning, I stood staring through a large window into the Neonatal Intensive Care Unit (NICU), watching Matt gently stroke little Kate through the handholes of her isolette.

I thought, *How can this be happening? God, where are You?*

A woman standing next to me started a conversation.

"Do you have a baby in there?" she asked.

"Yes, my grandchild."

She remarked that her little boy was in there also, but he was much improved and would be released the next day.

Then she asked, "You're a Christian, aren't you?"

I certainly didn't feel much like a Christian at that point, so I muttered, "I guess so." But to myself I thought, *A lot of good it's done me.*

She asked, "Have you prayed for Kate?"

"I don't know how to pray right now. Did you pray for your little boy?"

She quickly answered, "Yes, I did."

Then I asked, "How did you pray? I don't seem to be able to get any words out. Each time I try to pray, I'm just overwhelmed with emotion and frustration."

"Oh, honey, I just prayed for mercy! And I'll pray for mercy for your Kate."

Maybe her prayers will get better answers than mine, I thought to myself.

I never saw that lady again, but early the next morning as Glen and I made a return trip to San Diego after having gone back to our home to gather clothing for a prolonged stay, I noticed my mother's Bible sitting on the car seat next to me.

Well, Lord, I don't believe in the hunt and peck system, but I can't think of any verses that would help me just now. So I'm going to let the Bible fall open, and if You have anything that will help me, please let me find it.

The Bible fell open to Psalm 103 and my eyes were fixed on verse 17. Here is the Heavilin paraphrase—and emphasis—of the verse, "The Lord will show *mercy* to the righteous and to their children's children."

For the next few months, when God brought Kate to my mind, I just prayed *Mercy.*

The first brainwave test on little Kate showed considerable brain damage. A few weeks later the tests showed there was definitely damage, but it did not appear to be as severe as in the previous test. At six months, the test showed "No brain damage at all."

At two and a half, our little Kate was able to take a puzzle of the United States apart, put it back together by herself, and tell us the name of every state! She started teaching herself to read at three and a half—there is no question, God was abundantly merciful to us.

Just recently I heard a tape by Bob Mumford discussing the word *mercy*. By observing the various incidences in Scripture where people asked for and received mercy from Christ, Mr. Mumford concluded that the word *mercy* entails salvation, healing, forgiveness, cleansing, deliverance, and miracles. With this understanding, I am reminded how often God saw my need and answered my prayer by showing me mercy.

As I walk through various Egypts, I reflect on God's faithfulness to me, which gives me confidence that once again He will rescue me and show me His sovereign mercy.

With reflection also comes understanding. As we look back on our past behaviors, it is easy to see what we should have done. But as we reflect on God's actions, it is often possible to see that He knew what He was doing after all. He doesn't need hindsight!

When our son Jimmy died at seven weeks of age of crib death, I kept wondering, *What have I done wrong? Why would God allow this to happen to me?*

Tom, our doctor, had recently returned from serving as a missionary in India. When an Indian national came to visit Tom, he brought him to our home to meet us. Since the Indian man had also experienced a great deal of suffering, Tom felt we would benefit from knowing each other. The man came into our house wearing a long white tunic and sandals, and I felt as though God Himself were walking into our living room.

The man took my hand, held it very gently, and said, "What a privilege to meet someone God could *trust* with such a sorrow."

The concept still boggles my mind. We look at suffering and pain as punishment, but God is proud of us as His children. Perhaps some of the suffering and difficulties I walk through are put there so that I can discover what God already knew. He can trust me! What a humbling thought.

As the apostle Peter wrote: "Beloved, do not think it strange concerning the fiery trial which is to try you, as though some strange thing happened to you; but rejoice to the extent that you partake of

Christ's sufferings, that when His glory is revealed, you may also be glad with exceeding joy" (1 Peter 4:12–13).

Dear Jesus, Thank You for never giving up on me. Thank You for seeing potential where I see none. Let me see myself through Your eyes. In Jesus' Name. Amen.

The Real Me

I sit at Your feet
    Into Your face I stare.
The real meaning of me
    Is someplace in there.

I fix my eyes on You,
    My reflection then I see.
The image cast from Your eyes
    Is not my picture of me.

When I look into my mirror,
    I see everything that's wrong.
When I look into Your eyes,
    I see someone you've made strong.

My sin, my failures, my shame,
    Are not shadowed in Your face.
I see the cross, the pain You bore
    Radiating to me Your grace.
                         M.W.H. 1992

Practicing His Presence

1. What Egypt are you in right now? Ask God to cause you to reflect upon the Egypts He has brought you out of in times past.

_____

_____

_____

_____

2. Ask Him to help you to use the past Egypts to give you courage in the present one.

_____

_____

_____

_____

3. Thank Him for His promised deliverance.

_____

_____

_____

_____

23

Correction

When we listen to God's voice, He will be faithful in convicting us of our sins and showing us how we should correct our walk.

Not too long ago I received a phone call from a young mother. She and I had prayed together often and she had received much emotional and spiritual healing from God. This particular day, however, she was very upset.

She said, "I need to see you as soon as possible. I just blew it with my daughter. We got involved in a very heated discussion. I said things I should not have said. She was so upset that she left the house. I have to find out where all of my rage is coming from when I try to discipline my children."

Later that day, after she described the situation in more detail to me, we sat quietly in prayer, listening for what God wanted to say. Very quickly, my friend saw herself as a little girl and heard her own mother demeaning her just the way she had demeaned her daughter.

Although I had a strong feeling how God was going to direct her, I have learned to sit quietly, although not always patiently, and wait for God Himself to speak to the individual.

After the lady processed what she saw, she began to realize when she was a little girl, she couldn't fight back or defend herself when her mother verbally abused her. Since she couldn't release her feelings, the rage began to build inside of her. Now when she disciplined her own children, she was big enough to take control, but the control displayed itself in her own form of verbal abuse toward her children.

She sat there and allowed herself to feel all of the hurt and pain that little child had buried so deep within herself. Eventually she was able to speak out in prayer and say, "Mom, I forgive you for verbally abusing me when I was a little girl. You hurt me so badly, but I am now leaving you and your sin at the cross for Jesus to deal with. I love you and forgive you."

Next, my friend talked to Jesus and said, "Jesus, even though I now understand where my rage comes from, that doesn't excuse my behavior toward my children. I confess my sin to you and ask you to forgive me."

Very quickly after receiving forgiveness from Jesus, this dear mother realized she had to go home, find her child, and ask her to forgive her for her verbal abuse. She shared with me later that as she talked with her daughter and told her how God had dealt with her that evening, the daughter's hardness and belligerent spirit melted away.

Jesus knew there would be days we would "blow it," but He still devised a plan whereby we could be rescued: "He has delivered us from the power of darkness and conveyed us into the kingdom of the Son of His love, in whom we have redemption through His blood, the forgiveness of sins" (Col. 1:13-14).

I have discovered that when we are listening to God, He not only corrects us in the area of our sin, but He may also want to correct our perception of things that have happened to us either presently or in childhood.

A few years ago I was reading a book on emotional healing prayer and as the author suggested, I asked God to show me any areas in my past that were not resolved and were holding me back from becoming the woman He wanted me to be. I thought I knew most of the situations God would show me, but I was very surprised when God brought a familiar childhood scene to my mind.

I was about three years old, and I lived with my parents in a home my father had built. While our house had some very nice features such as beautiful hardwood floors throughout, which my mom waxed and polished frequently, there was no indoor plumbing in our house. I remember that the kitchen was equipped with a slop bucket, which was a white enamel bucket used to hold garbage and waste water, and that the mirrored medicine chest was mounted on the wall above the bucket. While my mom was gone one evening and my dad was home with me, I decided to get all cleaned up so that I could look pretty when Mommy came home. I washed my face, put on a clean dress, and combed my hair. Just to make sure I looked pretty, I placed my tiny, little three-year-old feet on the rim of the slop bucket so I could stand high enough to look into the mirror.

I looked into the mirror and said to myself, "You're pretty." Just about that time I lost my balance, tipping over the bucket, causing its contents to pour out onto the freshly waxed hardwood floors. Although my gentle, peaceful dad usually did not react rashly, watching that dirty waste water run over those beautiful floors caused him to suddenly pick me up by the arms, swing me back and forth, and mop the floor up with the lower portion of my body.

Although this story has not been kept secret in our family, whenever it was mentioned, the family's reaction, including mine, was "How embarrassing for Daddy." I grew up feeling sorry for my dad, but I never considered my own feelings. It is true that his reaction was not typical for him and he was very embarrassed. However, when I asked God to show me memories that were not resolved, He brought this memory to my mind immediately. But this time, God allowed me to see the event from His perspective. I realized the little three-year-old was devastated and humiliated, and she felt very ashamed and unattractive. I then realized since that time I have had difficulty believing I am physically attractive. As God walked me through that event of more than fifty years ago, He allowed me to see Jesus pick me up, wipe me off, brush my hair, look me in the eye, and say, "You are pretty."

I did not realize what a strong effect the recalling of this memory had on me until the next time I stood in front of the mirror and began to brush my hair. I looked at the woman in the mirror and was able to say, "I think you're pretty." God had changed my perspective of myself. He had saved the understanding of that scene for me until I was ready to receive it from His perspective. It is my prayer that I will always be able to see people and events from God's point of view.

I'm Just a Little Girl

"I'm sorry,
  I didn't mean to make a mess.
I just wanted to be pretty
  For Mommy, I guess."

I'm all wet and dirty.
  I must have been bad.
I stand all alone,
  Feeling shameful and sad.

With the eyes of my heart
  I see Jesus is there.
He scoops me into His arms,
  All my shame to bear.

He brushes my hair,
  Gently lifts my chin,
Until my downcast eyes
  Are fixed on Him.

I cry, "Oh Jesus, I'm sorry.
  I feel so alone."
He whispers, "Fear not, my child;
  My love will be shown.

Take My hand, stand tall
  And walk facing Me.
My beautiful, pretty one,
  You'll always be."
                    M.W.H. 1992

Practicing His Presence

1. As you begin to write your prayer to God today, if you desire
   to know the truth, ask Him to show you where your
   perceptions have been incorrect. Listen as He speaks to you
   and let Him walk through the scenes with you. Write them
   down with as much detail as you can. Ask Jesus to help you
   accept His perspective of each situation and give Him
   permission to work in you accordingly. Listen as He speaks.

   _____

   _____

   _____

   _____

24

Direction

As we wait on the Lord and listen for His voice, He promises that He will give us direction: "I will instruct you and teach you in the way you should go;/I will guide you with My eye" (Ps. 32:8).

Our tendency seems to be to listen and hear His direction very clearly on big issues. If you have received a call to full-time Christian service, you probably would be able to tell me exactly when you received that call. Usually we can relate those special times to a series of events or special Scripture verses. God manages to get our attention when it comes to the "big issues."

But what about the daily, ordinary events of life? Do we really listen for God's voice; do we pay attention even when we hear Him; or do we just muddle through life, hit or miss, hoping we're doing the right thing?

Our God is interested in our days, not just our years; in our minutes, not just our hours. He is speaking all of the time. I believe that we simply don't listen or even ask for direction on daily events until things don't go right or we're in trouble.

God is so interested in every minute detail of my life, that I believe He is even interested in who sits next to me on airplanes. Each time I get on the plane, I just wait to see if I'm going to get to sleep on this trip, or if I'm going to have a divine appointment. I learned to be prepared for the divine appointments early on in my speaking ministry.

One day as I was walking through the airport, having checked my bags at the curb, I sensed the Lord saying to me, "You don't have books with you and you are going to need one on this plane."

My first response was, "Lord, I was hoping I could sleep on this trip." And I kept on walking toward my gate.

However, I heard God's voice again, more persistent this time. "You don't have any books with you. You had better go back and get one out of your suitcase."

Since the thought wasn't going away, I reluctantly turned around, went back out to the curb, got some copies of *Roses in December* out of my bag, and proceeded back through the airport to my gate.

As I got on the plane, I looked around and thought, *I don't see anyone who looks as if he or she needs a book on grief. Maybe that wasn't God's voice after all.*

As the plane started to take off, however, the gentleman sitting next to me looked out the window and commented almost to himself, "I wish California had had better weather while I was here."

I casually asked, "Were you here on business or pleasure?"

He turned to me, started to answer, hesitated, and then began to cry.

I put my hand on his arm and said, "Sir, can you tell me what has been going on in your life lately?"

He tried to wipe away his tears, looking a little embarrassed, and said, "I don't know why I'm telling you this, but I came to California to bury my eighteen-year-old son!"

I reached into my briefcase, pulled out a book, and said, "Sir, I don't know if you believe in divine appointments, but you've just had one!"

I spent the next three hours listening to this man pour out his heart to me. As we parted, I was so thankful I could leave him with a book in his hand that would provide him with many of the answers he so desperately needed.

While the Lord often gives me direction concerning my interaction with someone else, He also gives me very decisive direction about myself.

This past December I was on a week-long speaking tour through Atlanta and several surrounding Georgia towns. The day I arrived in Atlanta, I had already been on the road several days. When my plane landed, I had approximately two and a half hours to get my baggage, be driven to the hotel, unpack my bags, press my clothes, and be ready to speak to about five hundred ladies that evening. First, my bags were delayed in arriving. Then we got lost on the way to the hotel, so much of my already limited time was consumed. After I got to the hotel, I received word that the books I had ordered had not arrived—which meant I was giving my testimony, entitled "Roses in December," but I didn't have a single *Roses in December* book available to sell. Much of the little time I had left was taken up in phone calls to my husband and my publisher. By that time I was in tears.

Finally I did what I should have done in the first place: I stopped to pray and listen to my heavenly Father. I poured out my sad story to God and told Him how frustrated I was; then I let Him talk to me. He didn't say much, just a few words, but that's all I needed to hear. Jesus said to me, "You are My child. Now act like it!" I quickly went into the bathroom, washed my face, got all dressed up, and went to that banquet to represent my heavenly Father to the best of my ability. Just in those few words Jesus reminded me that my joy and peace were not dependent on the arrival of a box of books, but my joy and peace were dependent on Jesus Christ, my eternal supplier of joy and peace!

Jesus will speak through other people, through circumstances and events, through His Word, and through the thoughts and ideas He puts into our minds. The latter is the vehicle most ignored and neglected today. We have almost let the church collective convince us that God will not speak to us personally but only through external means. Christians often imply we are a little "strange" if we claim to hear God's voice or see His face.

As I was reading through Jim Elliot's journal I was delighted to read his comments on this subject.

Psalm 27:8 "When thou saidst, Seek ye my face; my heart said unto thee, Thy face, Lord will I seek" yesterday seemed to explain what I have experienced lately of an inner "answering voice" which laughs at my doubts, argues against my bickerings with the Spirit. That word says, "My heart said for thee. . . ." I have known this—my own heart speaking for God, in His place. It calls me "child," "son of my love," "Jimmy"—strange and not at all static, but I have sensed it nonetheless real.[1]

As I am learning to train my ear to hear His voice, I realize God has an opinion on nearly everything I do. I do not mean we cannot make a move without getting a special delivery word from the Lord, although some people do operate that way. However, I do believe every good thought that comes into my head is guided by God because I am His child. I have asked the Holy Spirit to control and guide me; therefore, if a thought passes through my mind, *Encourage Marita today*, or *Call Irene*, I follow through.

Years ago a teacher of a women's Bible study I attended warned the group, "We must guard against a calloused conscience." How true that is! I have prayed many times that God would keep my conscience tender and sensitive, that I might respond immediately if I start to walk into a compromising situation.

As Christians who are seeking to hear God's voice, I think we should also pray, "God, please help me guard against a calloused, sterile, unresponsive mind."

How sad it would be if the Lord had to say of us, "Because you have done all these works . . . I spoke to you, rising up early and speaking, but you did not hear, and I called you, but you did not answer" (Jer. 7:13).

Practicing His Presence

1. Father, I am listening. I give You permission to speak to me through my mind. Please protect me from a calloused, sterile, unresponsive mind. With Samuel, I say, "Speak, LORD, Your servant is listening" (1 Sam. 3:10 NIV).

_____

_____

_____

_____

25

Inspection

All through this book, I have repeatedly emphasized the importance of knowing the God of Scripture and of checking everything we learn and every decision we make against His Word. We should be constantly learning and growing, but always inspecting our new thoughts and ideas. This is especially true in the area of listening prayer. I believe with all of my heart that God is speaking to each of His children individually and each of us can hear His voice. I also believe Satan is very capable of counterfeiting God's voice, so we must always test what we hear.

Job asked, "Does not the ear test words/And the mouth taste its food?" (Job 12:11). We can never be passive as Christians. We should be constantly running new thoughts and new information through the filter of God's Word to check their authenticity.

When I first began to receive the concepts of listening prayer—God would speak to me through my mind and I could write down what He said to me—I was very cautious and I examined these new concepts carefully. So far when I have heard what I recognized to be God's voice, I have heard nothing that would be contrary to Scripture, but I still check out what I hear.

Another confirmation God gave me was that others of God's people around the country were also hearing God speak to them in a similar way and He was telling them things that were consistent with what He was sharing with me.

Then as I began to read great men of prayer such as Oswald Chambers, C. S. Lewis, and C. H. Spurgeon, I discovered they heard God speak to them, too. And I thought I had discovered something new and revolutionary!

For me, after I have checked with Scripture and conferred with godly people of the past and present, if I'm still uncertain, my final checkpoint is Glen. Glen is very steady and well-founded in the things of God and I have confidence in his judgment. I have shared every new concept on listening prayer and prayer for emotional healing with him. Often he will have to think about my ideas for a day or two, and then he lets me know if he thinks I am staying on track. So far, he has endorsed all of the things I have been learning about prayer.

In any area, but especially in the area of biblical concepts, it is very wise to have a good inspection process in place for yourself. Too often the tendency today is to "do our own thing" and pull away from being accountable to anyone else for our thinking or our actions.

Peter Wagner examined accountability in relation to personal prayer intercessors:

> There is some justification for the fear some pastors have of personal intercession. They may not have thought it through in detail, but intuitively pastors realize that when they begin to relate to personal intercessors they move into a deeper level of vulnerability and accountability than before. This is not just imagination; it is a fact. Personal prayer partners make your life become much more of an open book.

I have mentioned that John Maxwell of Skyline Wesleyan Church has a team of 100 men who are committed to intercede for him and his ministry. I have visited the church several times and know some of his prayer partners personally. One of them is Dick Hausam who has received a special assignment from God to focus his prayers on John's moral life. John is on the road about as much as an NBA basketball player. He is no more exempt from temptation than any other man in his 40s. But almost every Sunday, Dick will approach John and say,

"How did it go this week?" John replies, "It went real well, but I don't know how it would have gone if you hadn't prayed for me."[1]

We need not fear stepping out into new territory in our Christian life as long as we always check our ideas out with Scripture and as long as we have a good accountability system around us that will help keep us on track.

Occasionally when we are listening to God speak to us, He will tell us something about someone else. We have to be especially careful when we receive thoughts about other people.

Several years ago, I made an entry in my journal, "Dear Lord, You know how badly Mellyn and Mike want a baby. They have been married seven years now. Please allow them to have a baby."

After I made that entry, every few days I wrote, "Jesus, please don't forget Mellyn." That was just my way of tugging at the hem of His garment to remind Him of our desire and need.

One day as I was praying and listening, I heard Jesus say, "Mellyn will be pregnant this year."

I thought, *Now what am I supposed to do with this?*

Finally, with a shaky hand I wrote down what I heard, "Mellyn will be pregnant this year." But I wrote it down in pencil so if I wasn't hearing right, I could erase it!

Each day after that, I thanked the Lord in faith for what I had heard. Then I wondered, *Should I tell Mellyn?* When I asked the Lord about it, the verse came to my mind, "But Mary kept all these things and pondered them in her heart" (Luke 2:19). I believed God would let me know if a time came that I should tell Mellyn, and I determined to wait until then.

A few months after that as I talked with Mellyn on the phone she told me that they had started attending a new church of only about seventy people. The pastor of the church stopped by to visit them and asked Mike if there was anything he could pray about for them.

Mellyn said, "Mom, you know we don't talk about this much, so I was really surprised when Mike said to this pastor we hardly knew, 'Sure you can pray for us. We want a baby.'"

The pastor prayed for them right there, and Mellyn said, "Each time he sees me, he looks at me and says 'Well—any news?'"

This man had true faith that his prayers were going to be answered.

Then Mellyn went on to tell me about Mother's Day in this little church. All of the children came in to the meeting room and gave their mothers violets. Mellyn was one of the few women in this small congregation who did not receive a flower. She related to me how difficult that was for her.

But then she added, "At the end of the service the pastor called me up front and gave me a violet. Then he said, 'Mellyn, I'm giving this to you in faith believing that next year you'll qualify for it!'"

This man's faith overwhelmed me, and I thought *Wow, and he doesn't even have an eraser!*

At that point, I felt comfortable in sharing with Mellyn what I had written in my journal several months before. We were able to pray and commit our desires to the Lord, put our trust in Him, and thank Him for the promises I had received.

About a month later while I was traveling in Michigan I checked my messages and there was a message from Mellyn. "Mom, would you give me a call? You can even call me at work if you want to."

I said to Glen, "She must be pregnant!"

When I called, I said, "When's it due?" And she said, "February!" Now as I look at our precious little Christian, I am reminded of God's faithfulness. First, He let me be one of the first to know that a baby was promised, He gave me wisdom to ponder His words in my heart, and then He let me be Christian's "Grammie."

What a wonderful God we serve!

Listen, My Child

Listen, My child,
    and I will speak.
Affection I'll give
    when My voice you seek.

Reflect on past scenes,
    and new visions receive.
Correction is hard,
    but I'll not deceive.

Direction will come
    as you yield to My choice.
Inspection is wise
    to assure it's My voice.

Be still, wait on Me.
    You have nothing to fear.
Listen, My child,
    and My voice you'll hear.

M.W.H. 1992

Practicing His Presence

1. Has God given you some prophetic thoughts? Write them down here.

_____

_____

_____

_____

2. Now check them against Scripture. Write down the Scripture that confirms or contradicts your thoughts.

_____

_____

_____

_____

3. Check your thoughts out with wise counselors. Write down their responses.

_____

_____

_____

_____

4. Do you have someone to whom you are ultimately accountable? Share your thoughts with them.

_____

_____

_____

_____

Part

6

THE PRODUCT OF PRAYER

26

A Quieted Spirit

As I have read and reread the pages of this handbook on prayer, I realize some of the topics that would normally appear in a book on prayer are not here. I have not discussed much about how to get our prayers answered or why they don't seem to be answered. Although I have emphasized the importance of a personal quiet time, I have left it between you and God as to how yours should be. While I imagine I could write a section, if not an entire book, on each of those topics, they have been well covered many times over in other books, and I did not want these issues to be the focal point of this book. I have discovered that as I have learned to be quiet before the Lord, He has instructed me in each of these areas, and He will do the same for you. But the secret was learning to be quiet before Him. I simply want the message of this book to be: Pray and listen; pray and listen. Don't give up; keep listening and you will hear His voice.

I have been alone in a hotel for two days trying to finish this book. I have been asking the Lord what kind of product we should be looking for as we develop an effective prayer life.

First, the Lord let me see that as I pray, I bring joy to Him and to myself. As I touch His face and look into His eyes, He becomes real to me, and my own existence is validated. I accept myself as I become whole in Him.

I have been a Christian for over fifty years and have sat under the teaching of many notable and gifted pastors and teachers. In spite of all of my learning, however, I have often struggled with how God really feels about me. Until three years ago, I never dreamed I could actually hear in my mind, God the Father, the Creator of the entire universe, say, "Marilyn Heavilin, I love you!" I still cannot even write that statement without having the tears stream down my cheeks. *He* loves me! He *loves* me! He loves *me*!

When I was able to receive those words and let them permeate every cell of my body, my spirit became calmer. I became quiet before Him. My attitude about me changed, enough that others have noticed.

I work with many beautiful, talented, creative, and exciting women who are on the staff of CLASS (Christian Leaders, Authors, and Speakers Seminars). In my prayer time one day God let me see that when I pictured the staff all lined up on the stage, I could see Florence, Marita, Betty, and Bonnie. Although they are all different in stature and physical appearance, in my picture they were all equal. Then the Lord let me see that as I put myself in the picture, previously from my point of view, I was only about two inches high. Then Jesus showed me as I have been able to believe Him and receive His love unconditionally, my picture has changed. Now as I look at the picture of the staff, we are all equal, even me! For me, one of the products of developing a satisfying personal prayer life is that I can now stand tall before the Lord and before His people because I know *He loves me*.

Through prayer, I have also learned to depend on the Lord for simple needs, just as I would rely on a human friend. This week, while trying to finish up this manuscript, my computer went bonkers and I couldn't get it to do anything. It just seemed to freeze up. I tried pushing a few buttons, but nothing happened.

Now, my understanding of computers is very limited. Since my husband is a computer expert, I have always depended on him to bail me out of any crisis. My first thought was, *I'll call Glen and he'll get me out of this mess.* Then I realized Glen was out of town and unreachable. So my next thought was, *I'll just sit here and cry.*

Finally, I realized I hadn't prayed about my situation. So I just stopped and said, *Lord, I need your help. How are You with computers? I have obviously pushed the wrong button somewhere along the line, and now I don't know what to do.*

I sat quietly for a moment and then that still, small voice said in my mind, *Turn on your laptop computer. Since you have the manuscript on there, too, you will be able to compare the commands and see what you have done wrong.*

Within a minute I discovered my mistake, corrected it, and was back in business. Then I stopped and talked to my heavenly Father.

Dear Jesus, thank You for being so patient with me. Thanks for even understanding computers. Thank You also for helping me mature in You. In the middle of my mess, the panic only lasted for a moment, and then my thoughts turned to You. But at least I'm doing better, aren't I, Lord? Father, I want to get to the point that my very first thought in the middle of a dilemma is Pray. *But at least I'm doing better than I would have done a year ago. Thank You for quieting my mind. I love You, Jesus. Amen.*

My friend Kathy called me the other day to report how God had taught her to listen to His voice. She recalled:

My son's twelfth birthday was last week. We worked very hard to make it special, but Austin was very disappointed his dad and I couldn't afford to give him the birthday gifts he thought he deserved. He became very depressed because his bike wasn't as nice as his best friend's was. Austin was filled with anger and frustration over all he felt he lacked. It hurt me to see how discontented he had become, how filled with the flesh instead of the Spirit.

As I prayed about it, I asked the Lord what I could do to make Austin happy. The Lord spoke to my heart and said, "Kathy, you can't do it. This is between Me and your son. Trust me."

Then I got a call at work from Austin. I thought he was going to complain about something. Instead there was excitement in his voice. "Mom, guess what? I just picked up my Bible and was reading in James, chapter 3 and this is what it says: 'If your heart is full of bitter jealousy and selfishness, it is from the devil himself! But God's wisdom is kind and peaceful and doesn't cause trouble and say mean things and instead has a thankful heart.' It says you should pray and God will take those bad things away and give you good things in your life and in your heart."

Then he said, "Mom, I'm sorry and thank you for all the things you do for me, and I'm thankful to even have a bike!" Words to warm a mother's heart. All I could do was cry with joy! As the Lord had quieted my spirit and I had been willing to trust God with my son and his poor attitude, then God was free to work.

As I have learned to sit quietly before the Father, He has truly restored my soul. He wants to do the same thing for you. Once you have heard His voice and looked into His face, other aspects of prayer fall into place. I know He hears me, but as I look into His face my only desire is for His perfect will. Therefore, I can trust His answer and His timing. I no longer have to struggle and wonder if I prayed right or if I asked correctly. I just place my petitions in my Father's lap and leave the rest to Him. Through listening to His voice, He has produced a quieted spirit in me:

> The LORD is my shepherd;
> I shall not want.
> He makes me to lie down in
> green pastures;
> He leads me beside the still
> waters.
> He restores my soul.
> (Ps. 23:1–3)

Practicing His Presence

1. As you sit quietly before Him today, first write down the picture you have of yourself. Then ask Jesus to show you His picture of you. *Christian   Christian Mom, Sister, Wife, Grandma, Writer — Lord help me to exhibit Christ-like characteristics in all my roles!*

2. If there is anything condemning in the picture, know that it is not from God. Renounce the condemning pictures, and wait quietly until God's picture comes through. Write down what you see.

   _____

   _____

   _____

   _____

3. Today ask Him to quiet your mind, restore your soul, and correct your perception of yourself as you quietly wait on Him.

   _____

   _____

   _____

   _____

27

A Quickened Mind

Recently the Lord showed me that as I spend time in prayer with Him, I become wise because He gives me insight. I become alert.

As Christians, our minds must be clear so we can see the real issues. Our minds should be alert to God's quickening. We should not have dull minds that just let things go drifting by. We need to be clear-minded and self-controlled so that we can face the problems of life and pray.

Second Timothy 1:7 states, "For God has not given us a spirit of fear, but of power and of love and of a sound mind." One of the greatest things we need in the world today is people with sound minds. Most decisions being made in our country, in our families, and unfortunately even in our churches are not being produced from sound minds. We need people who can think clearly and think according to God's Scripture.

This should be our confidence:

> For the LORD gives wisdom;
> From His mouth come knowledge and understanding;
> He stores up sound wisdom for the upright;
> He is a shield to those who walk uprightly;
> He guards the paths of justice,

And preserves the way of His saints.
(Prov. 2:6-8)

Our minds need to be controlled by God so that when decisions and difficulties come to us, we can filter them through God's perspective, not man's perspective. His thoughts are not naturally our thoughts.

This past year Glen and I received a letter from Jennifer Eshleman, the daughter of Paul and Kathy Eshleman, longtime friends of ours who are on the staff of Campus Crusade for Christ. Jennifer was in a very serious motorcycle/bus accident.

Jennifer shared her remembrances of the accident:

At the site of the accident I was left lying on the street, my leg seeming to be ripped open and something looking very "wrong" about my foot underneath my sock. There I was for 25 minutes before help arrived. I screamed. I remember the scream—I thought I would die. Pain! Excruciating pain! Shooting up and down my leg. I yelled.

And then I heard a voice—the voice of the Lord—saying to me, "Jennifer, be still and know that I am God. It's okay. Calm down. I'm here. I haven't left you alone. I'm sorry this happened—oh, so sorry. But I'm still God, and I love you. Be still, Jennifer. I'm here—so close to you." I fell backward into the arms of a special friend with me and endured the pain with my heavenly Father by my side—not being inactive, but being God. At times when I cry out, "Where are You?" I have that special confidence that the God who was there assuring me of His presence from the first moments of the accident isn't going to leave.

Jennifer experienced what Scripture has promised: "But to be spiritually minded is life and peace" (Rom. 8:6). Even in the midst of a very painful trauma, Jennifer let God control her mind, and she was able to rest in Him. Through spending time in prayer, we can learn to live expectantly. We can become alert to God working all around us.

Chambers explained it this way:

When through Jesus Christ we are rightly related to God, we learn to watch and wait, and wait wonderingly. "I wonder how God will answer this prayer." "I wonder how God will answer the prayer of the Holy Ghost that's praying in me." "I wonder what glory God will bring to Himself out of the strange perplexities I am in." "I wonder what new turn His providence will take in manifesting Himself in my ways?"[1]

Now, that is the attitude of a quickened mind—one that recognizes that God is working and God is in control of our lives, and listens for His voice.

Recently a young man was referred to me because he had some questions about his temperament. I talked with him on the phone but never met him. Although he called regarding identifying his temperament, the Lord told me there was more. I asked him if he had any addictions, and he quickly answered no. But the Lord prompted me to ask him again. As I asked him the question again, he said, "Well, I have them, but they are under control."

Once that question was answered truthfully, the Lord allowed this young man and me to have a very honest and healing conversation and prayer time over the telephone. A quickened mind thinks to pray immediately, not as a last resort. Prayer will be the first response of one in tune with God.

Practicing His Presence

1. Let this be your prayer today: *Dear Father, quicken my mind to think of You and pray immediately when I am in a dilemma. Train my ear to hear Your voice. Amen.*

2. Think of times when praying was your last resort rather than your first thought.

   _____

   _____

   _____

   _____

   _____

   _____

3. List some decisions you have to make in the near future. Take time right now to discuss them with the Lord.

   _____

   _____

   _____

   _____

   _____

   _____

28

A Qualified Servant

Isaiah is probably one of the most quoted and mightily used prophets from the Old Testament, but recently something was brought to my attention that I had never noticed before about Isaiah. At first, Isaiah seemed to be simply mouthing what he saw in a vision. He used terms such as "hear the word of the LORD" (1:10); "Therefore the Lord says,/The LORD of hosts, the Mighty One of Israel" (1:24).

However, in chapter 6, Isaiah started out with these words: "In the year that King Uzziah died, I saw the Lord sitting on a throne, high and lifted up, the train of His robe filled the temple" (6:1).

Since I'm not a theologian, I haven't studied deeply what happened to Isaiah at this point, but apparently he saw Jesus. Even though he obviously believed in the God of Israel before that, when he "saw the Lord" something changed. From that point on in the book of Isaiah, Isaiah's prophecies are much more personal. "Then the LORD said to Isaiah" (7:3); "Moreover the LORD said to me" (8:1); "The LORD also spoke to me again" (8:5).

When Isaiah saw the Lord, his ministry changed. He no longer was performing his duties as a prophet in a robotic fashion, but his conversation with God became personal.

I can mark many growth points along my Christian journey, but I saw a picture of Jesus for the first time in the incident involving the slop bucket I refer to in chapter 23. That experience began a new level in my Christian walk. I saw Jesus, and He was holding *me*. My walk with Him became much more personal. At that moment I knew for sure Jesus loves me, not just in a collective sense that He loves all people who come to Him, but *He loves me*.

I love it when I discover something "new" and then my discovery is verified by someone's writing who lived long before me. I'm sure you've noticed I've quoted Oswald Chambers often in this book. Dear Oswald and I just seem to think alike very often, except that he expresses my feelings much better than I can. After I wrote my comments about Isaiah, I read this quote from Chambers: "Being saved and seeing Jesus are not the same thing. Many are partakers of God's grace who have never seen Jesus. When once you have seen Jesus, you can never be the same; other things do not appeal as they used to do."[1]

Along with Isaiah, as we develop an effective prayer life and as we see Jesus, we become confident of God's love for us, and we become usable servants. As we listen to His voice, study Scripture, and seek godly counsel, we will be ready for God to use us. When God speaks, we have to be willing to receive what He says if we want to become qualified servants.

I received this letter from Carol, a woman who attended one of my classes on prayer.

I had no idea exactly what your class would be like, but I went in expectation. As busy and hectic as the rest of the conference seemed to be, your class was an oasis where all could be set aside to hear from the Lord.

It's embarrassing because it reveals a thought I wasn't aware I was entertaining. My husband Bill is a professional golfer who was employed as a Head Pro until last October. He is also a playing pro and plays on the Golden State Tour and in PGA Chapter events in Southern California. The effects of the rain on the golf courses has made it impossible to play and so our income went to zero very quickly and our savings also. So, that night in your class, in the midst of the challenges of our financial situation His still, small voice said to my spirit, "I gave you Bill to love you in spite of yourself." I cried.

I had been focusing on our circumstances for a couple of weeks and I was miserable and doing a good job of making everyone else miserable, too. I had taken my eyes off things above. I had been blaming instead of trusting.

God's remark brought the problem home to me. I hope you can see how much this simple statement meant to me and how God put the responsibility of my actions back to me in a very unique and loving way.

As qualified servants we will see opportunities to represent our Lord, and we will be ready to serve. Recently I had to go to a lab to have a routine blood test. While I was waiting, I noticed a young woman sitting across from me who looked very distressed. Then I became aware of a child crying in one of the lab rooms. As the child's screams escalated, the young woman burst into tears. Without a second thought, I was able to move over next to her.

"I think you could use a hug," I said as I put my arm around her. She quickly laid her head on my shoulder. Then I asked, "Do you believe in prayer?"

Through her tears she nodded yes. I asked her the name of her child, and then I began to pray for Jeremy. I don't know much about Jeremy even now except he has had several surgeries and was facing another one. As I finished praying, Jeremy's daddy came out and placed the little boy in his mother's arms, and they were gone.

I sat there and prayed, *Thank You, Jesus for letting me represent You to this family today. Thank You for helping me be a qualified servant who was ready to be used by You today. Amen.*

To quote the prophet Isaiah once again:

Yet your teachers will not be moved into a corner anymore, but your eyes shall see your teachers. Your ears shall hear a word behind you, saying, "This is the way, walk in it," whenever you turn to the right hand or whenever you turn to the left. (Isa. 30:20–21)

Practicing His Presence

1. Are you a qualified servant? If not, what is holding you back?

_____

_____

_____

_____

2. What do you need to do to be "on call" for God?

_____

_____

_____

_____

3. Write Him a letter today and tell Him what you are willing to do to become a qualified servant.

_____

_____

_____

_____

_____

_____

29

A Quality of Life

It is my hope as you have gone through the studies and worksheets in this book that your perspective on prayer will have changed. I trust you now know an effective prayer life is attainable for you and that it is possible for you to dialogue with God. To me, prayer has become one of the most exciting parts of the Christian experience, not just a requirement of the Christian life or something I do when I'm in trouble. It is my prayer that would be true for you also.

If you have just read through the text but have not done the journal exercises, I urge you to go back through the book and complete the assignments. The questions in the worksheets are the very ones that helped me attain a satisfactory prayer experience. Some of them are thought-provoking and some will expose very painful areas in your life, but the results will be worth the effort. Give God a chance to become even more real in your life.

As I have studied, I have also learned God puts much more value on each individual prayer than I could ever imagine. As I looked up all the verses in the Bible on prayer, I found some verses really made me curious because I wasn't sure what they meant.

Revelation 5:8 mentions the four living creatures that John saw: ". . . the four living creatures and the twenty-four elders fell down before the Lamb, each having a harp, and golden bowls full of incense, which are the prayers of the saints." *Who are the saints whose prayers are referred to?* I wondered.

Revelation 8:3, "Then another angel, having a golden censer, came and stood at the altar. And he was given much incense, that he should offer it with the prayers of all the saints upon the golden altar which was before the throne." It doesn't say some, but "*all the saints,* on the golden altar before the throne" (emphasis mine). That means your prayers and mine are included in those golden bowls.

And then Revelation 8:4, "And the smoke of the incense, with the prayers of the saints, ascended before God from the angel's hand." I asked myself, *Why were they burning the prayers of the saints?*

I checked with Halley's Bible Commentary on these passages, and its interpretation was "The prayers of all the saints are weighed by the divine arbiter, as He charts the course of history." And then Halley's comment is, "What a light this sheds on prayer."[1]

I asked myself, *Could this mean that the Lord looks to see how many prayers are there, how many people are concerned about a given situation, and whether the people are praying the way they ought to be? Does that affect His answer?* Then my thoughts turned to James 5:16, "The effective, fervent prayer of a righteous man avails much." It is obvious God wants to know we are serious about our requests. If we mention something to Him once and never mention it again, He certainly could conclude our request was just a passing fancy rather than a true desire of our heart.

We need not be afraid to come before the throne of God often to remind Him of the intensity of our request and the desires of our heart.

A pastor-friend said he believes the Revelation passages teach that the "prayers of all are highly valued and not just heard, and that they are like love letters to the Lord." Have you considered each of your prayers to be "love letters to the Lord"?

When Glen and I were dating, much of our courtship was conducted through letters since he lived in Indiana and I lived in Michigan. I lived for the arrival of the mail each day. I hungrily read and reread each letter from my love; then I put each letter away in a special place. In fact, thirty-five years later, I still have the letters Glen wrote to me before we were married. Is it possible that our heavenly

Father treats our prayers as love letters? Could He savor each word as we savor words from the one we love? Then, as we save words from our loved one, does He save our prayers? I believe the answer is yes. We are His bride. His heart thrills when we talk with Him.

Have you ever gone to a party and discovered that everybody had made more of the party than you had? You were underdressed, and everybody else brought a present and you didn't. Then you think, *Oh, if they would have just let me know, I could have dressed up more. I could have made more fuss about this party. I would have brought a present. I wish I had realized how important this party was.*

I believe some of us will get to heaven, look around and say, "Those prayers really could have been answered. I just didn't offer them. They aren't here. They're missing. I didn't recognize their importance. I didn't know He was going to save them. I didn't know how special I am to Him. My spot looks rather empty. I wish I could get ready for this party all over again."

I hope as I look at those bowls, I'll be able to say, "There are my prayers. There are my prayers for my son-in-law, Mike, and my grandson, Christian, my granddaughter, Kate, my grandson, Nate, for all of my children, and look how God answered. Here are other prayers and this is what happened because of them. Oh, I remember when I prayed those prayers. My oh my, what beautiful presents they make in that bowl."

In that same Revelation passage our prayers are said to be offered as an incense to the Lord. My pastor-friend says, "The incense is the sweet-smelling savor, and worship and prayer should be a whole-body experience. This means as your prayers are offered up as a perfume to the Lord, you are worshiping with all of your senses."

Our prayers are precious to the Lord, and He's collected them all. My friend Marita and I run the Southern California Women's Retreat together. Often she receives phone calls which need to be passed on to me. When she calls, if I'm not home, each time she leaves a similar message, "Marilyn, Marilyn, here is a message about the retreat. Now that I've given it to you, I can get it off my desk and throw this piece of paper away." Once we have completed a task, we tend to forget it and move on to something else.

I always thought that was the way God treated my prayers. Now I realize God doesn't just answer my prayers and throw them in the heavenly wastebasket. He keeps them. He preserves them just as I've saved Glen's love letters. We're going to see them, and we're going to offer them as the ultimate worship, a sweet-smelling aroma to our God. I believe heaven will be perfumed with the aroma from our prayers.

Will yours be there?

No prayer is too small or unimportant. They all matter to our heavenly Father. It doesn't matter so much *how we pray*, but it matters immensely *that we pray*.

And some day, when you look at that golden bowl, I pray that your spot will be full and overflowing: Jesus said, "Pray and [do] not lose heart" (Luke 18:1).

And remember, don't come to the party without any presents!

My Presents for Him

"I've enjoyed all your presents," He said
as He walked me to His golden bowl.
"What presents?" I asked,
trying hard not to appear slow.

"Why, the presents you sent ahead.
The prayers of praise and thanksgiving.
The prayers of your needs and desires.
The ones about everyday living."

"But, Lord!" I exclaimed, "I almost felt guilty
whenever I prayed.
I was sure I was bothering You
with requests that I made."

"But," He said, "through your prayers,
I saw your heart.
You showed your concern for others,
and a desire to do your part.

I loved it when you spoke to Me,
when you declared your love;
when you shared your dreams
with your Father above."

"Oh Father, it's taken so long
for me to understand
That as I pray, I'm placing
precious gifts in Your hand.

I now see as I give You
my presents of prayer,
You place them in the golden bowls
and save them for me there.

Oh, Jesus, if I'd only known,
I would have sent more."
"Take heart, My child, I'm giving you
time to restore.

Talk to Me, child;
and don't delay.
Send your presents ahead. Together
we'll open them someday."

M.W.H. 1993

Practicing His Presence

1. Are there prayers you have failed to pray? List those prayers here.

_____

_____

_____

_____

2. Why have you failed to pray those prayers?

_____

_____

_____

_____

3. Place yourself before the Father and give Him your presents, the prayers you haven't prayed before. He will give you courage. Pray and don't lose heart.

_____

_____

_____

_____

Notes

To the Reader

1. Oswald Chambers, *My Utmost for His Highest* (Westwood, N.J.: Barbour and Company, 1963), February 12. (Note: All quotations by Oswald Chambers in this book are used by the permission of the Oswald Chambers Publications Assn., Ltd., and Discovery House Publishers, Box 3566, Grand Rapids, MI 49501. All rights reserved.)

Chapter 1: Know the Principal of Prayer

1. Dick Purnell, *A 31-Day Experiment: Knowing God by His Names* (Nashville: Thomas Nelson, 1993). Used by permission.

Chapter 2: Know His Power

1. *Oswald Chambers: The Best from All His Books, Vol. 1* (Nashville: Oliver-Nelson Books, 1987), 255.
2. Ibid.

Chapter 3: Know His Purpose

1. Chambers, *The Best from All His Books, Vol. 1*, 243.

Chapter 4: Know His Protection

1. Charles H. Spurgeon, *Spurgeon at His Best: Over Twenty-Two Hundred Striking Quotations from the World's Most Exhaustive & Widely Read Sermon Series*, comp. Tom Carter (Grand Rapids: Baker Book House, 1988), 57.
2. *Oswald Chambers: The Best from All His Books, Vol. 2*, (Nashville: Oliver-Nelson Books, 1989), 232.

Chapter 5: Know His Presence

1. Chambers, *My Utmost for His Highest*, 30.

2. Elisabeth Elliot, ed., *The Journals of Jim Elliot* (Old Tappan, N.J.: Revell, 1978), 212.
3. Chambers, *My Utmost for His Highest*, March 17.

Chapter 6: Distractions
1. Spurgeon, *Spurgeon at His Best*, 143.
2. Ibid., 146.
3. Chambers, *The Best from All His Books, Vol. 1*, 248.

Chapter 10: Disbelief
1. *God's Victorious Army Bible*, Spiritual Warfare Reference Edition II, comp. Morris Cerullo (San Diego, 1989), 1100.
2. Spurgeon, *Spurgeon at His Best*, 147-148.

Chapter 17: Inspiration
1. Chambers, *The Best from All His Books, Vol. 1*, 179.
2. Sue Monk Kidd, *When the Heart Waits* (San Francisco: Harper & Row, 1990), as excerpted in *alive now!*, January/February, 1992.
3. "The Eloquent Sounds of Silence," *Time*, January 25, 1993, 74.
4. Spurgeon, *Spurgeon at His Best*, 145.

Chapter 18: Instruction
1. Chambers, *The Best from All His Books, Vol. 1*, 247.

Chapter 19: Intercession
1. Chambers, *The Best from All His Books, Vol. 1*, 260.
2. Ibid., 261.
3. C. Peter Wagner, *Prayer Shield*, Prayer Warrior Series (Ventura, CA: Regal Books, 1992), 104-105. Used by permission.
4. Ibid., 106.
5. Chambers, *The Best from All His Books, Vol. 1*, 261.
6. Ibid., 244.
7. Ibid., 259.

Chapter 20: Separation
1. Spurgeon, *Spurgeon at His Best*, 145-146.

2. Chambers, *The Best From All His Books, Vol. 1*, 255.
3. C.S. Lewis, *Mere Christianity* (New York: Macmillan, 1978) 142–143.
4. Spurgeon, *Spurgeon at His Best*, 146.
5. Ibid.

Chapter 21: Affection
1. Spurgeon, *Spurgeon at His Best*, 123.

Chapter 24: Direction
1. Elliot, *The Journals of Jim Elliot*, 98.

Chapter 25: Inspection
1. Wagner, *Prayer Shield*, 110.

Chapter 27: A Quickened Mind
1. Chambers, *The Best from All His Books, Vol. 1*, 42.

Chapter 28: A Qualified Servant
1. Chambers, *My Utmost for His Highest*, April 9.

Chapter 29: A Quality of Life
1. Henry H. Halley, *Halley's Bible Handbook* (Grand Rapids, MI: Zondervan, 1964), 644.

About the Author

Marilyn Heavilin is a wife, mother, grandmother, former high school counselor, and a frequent speaker on the topics of grief, family life, child-rearing, and the problem of drinking drivers. She is recommended by the speakers' bureaus for Christian Leaders, Authors, and Speakers' Seminars (CLASS) and Mothers Against Drunk Drivers (MADD) and is a frequent speaker for Compassionate Friends, a support group for bereaved parents.

In addition to her own speaking commitments, Marilyn helps others improve their speaking skills through her staff position with CLASS. She and her husband, Glen, live in Redlands, California.

Marilyn can be contacted at

CLASS Speakers
1645 S. Rancho Santa Fe Road, Suite 102
San Marcos, CA 92069